D1559353

WHITE TALES

A Modern Look at Deer Hunting

By DAVE HENDERSON

Outdoors Today ● *Endicott, NY*

Dedicated to Mom. You always believed in me.
Thanks for being who you are.

Introduction

Since this is the first manifestation of what will hopefully be a fruitful and enjoyable association with you, the reader, good etiquette demands an introduction of sorts.

Now it would be nice to describe the author as a crack marksman, uncanny woodsman and sportsman of international renown. The truth of the matter, however, is that he is none of these things.

Oh, he can shoot better than average. And he does guide hunters professionally in the Rocky Mountains, so his woodsmanship passes muster. But he's been known to shoot slow when bucks run fast, gets more respect among the B Division shooters than the AA boys, and doesn't bring home the biggest buck in the county every year. In fact, like many of you, he's been known to spend more time behind a desk than afield.

The plaques on the wall are thus not awards for hunting or shooting but rather for writing about it with some degree of competence. Being able to make a living as a reporter isn't based on being an all-knowing expert on every topic. A good reporter instead knows where to find an expert and how to translate that man's expertise into readable prose. Suffice to say that your author's main claim to fame is that he knows lots of experts.

Please understand that during my formative days in this trade all self-respecting journalists regretted the use of the personal pronoun. Times and journalistic outlooks have changed, but I haven't. Apologies are offered, therefore, since the use of the first person singular is unavoidable in situations such as this.

Now well into my third decade as a professional journalist stationed in the verdant, rolling dairy country of upstate New York, I started as a newspaper hack. In the mid-1980s I forsook the security of a steady paycheck and paid health benefits to go on my own and today am a nationally syndicated newspaper outdoors columnist with United Press International and gun columnist with several national publications, including Buckmasters and Canadian Out-

The author at work.

doors Publications. That position has provided extraordinary hunting opportunities to experience and experts to tap.

This book includes adaptions of many of my award-winning articles and others from among the nearly 2,000 that I've sold over the years.

As mentioned above I consider myself to be a pretty ordinary outdoorsman. I hunt with a shotgun, compound bow, bolt-action and muzzleloading rifles and a 35mm camera.

Hell yes I envy those who have the disposable income, free time and sufficiently understanding family to hunt big bucks in Texas and a couple of western Canadian provinces every year, sandwiched around annual forays for elk and bear. While I know plenty of those types and admire their custom guns, expensive hunting leases and skewed priorities, I can find the same enjoyment and satisfaction hunting a familiar patch of woods in my home county, wearing Woolrich or fading Tru-Leaf and toting a pump shotgun or battle-scarred bow.

I have no binding allegiances to clubs, causes or brand names. I abhor politics and fear that lawmakers, in their understandable zeal to keep weapons out of the hands of hoodlums and not so understandable compulsion to sympathize with bunny-hugging activists, may in time threaten something that I see as a fine American heritage.

The sense of self-sufficiency provided by taking one's own meat has long been appealing to me. A freezer full of venison, fish fillets and birds is a far more meaningful trophy than any set of antlers on the wall.

The taxes and license fees that I pay for hunting and fishing help pay for the conservation of all wild creatures, not just those few hunted and fished. I thus make no apologies to any cocktail party philosophers for following a life deemed honorable since time immemorial.

If outside references are needed for a rounder picture, be advised that I am definitely not Politically Correct, drive only American vehicles and don't wear an earring. I've have never played Nintendo, couldn't tell you which rock group sings what and don't feel culturally deprived when I work or sleep through television's prime time hours. I'm addicted to caffeine, love shoot-'em-up Eastwood movies and am still innocent enough to think of the beverage when the word "coke" is dropped in casual conversation.

My spouse understands better than most what it is that makes a man forsake a warm bed to face dawn in a windswept treestand— and the need to keep a straight face when excuses abound for the latest missed shot. We live in a house where venison and wild birds provide the only red meat and fowl table fare, a situation to which my bride warmed nicely after a considerably shaky start two decades ago. I am still on a friendly terms with our child and will probably remain so as long as my television appearances don't conflict with Disney Channel programming.

On top of it all, I have spent most of my adult life getting paid to do things that any sensible man would happily do for free. This book is simply an extension of that good fortune and I look forward to sharing it with you.

—Dave Henderson

"HOW you hunt is not nearly as important as WHERE you hunt."   —Gene Wensel

Forward

The big-racked whitetail, the mossy-horned big guy that adorns virtually every outdoors magazine cover at least a few months each year, is the goal of every deer hunter. The sport hunting industry is based on the myth that it takes a knowledgable, well-equipped hunter to get that big buck.

The notion that guile and equipment are the big factors in taking a trophy buck are myths perpetuated by magazine articles—missives, by the way, to which I am an admitted and enthusiastic contributor. But let's not blame magazines. They're providing what we want—fodder to fuel the dreams. The purpose and usefulness of hunting magazines to a hunter is the same as "Playboy" or "Penthouse" to the average heterosexual male. It's entertaining and sometimes educational to look at and read. Damned stimulating, right? But Joe Average has got about as much chance of encountering and shooting that Boone & Crockett 12-pointer on the cover as he has seducing and landing in bed with the centerfold.

Yes, there are guys out there who devote their lives to hunting big bucks and are very successful. Some of them parlay their knowledge and experience into magazine stories, books, videos and fame. This allows Joe Average to identify with that success—despite the fact that Joe doesn't have the same time, resources, dedication or inclination as the author.

In short, we all want to be skillful hunters with the best equipment. But we've got to look past the glitter and realize that inordinate skill, special techniques and high tech equipment are very small factors in successful deer hunting.

Don't just take my word for it. Renowned bowhunting author-lecturer Gene Wensel notes in his seminars, "HOW you hunt is not nearly as important as WHERE you hunt." Well-known midwestern bowhunter Bob Fratzke makes it even clearer when he says, "If you want to take a big buck you've got to hunt where there are big bucks. The best hunter in the world isn't going to kill a big buck where there aren't any."

Taxidermists and outdoors writers constantly hear stories about the taking of big bucks. Of the hundreds of bucks I mounted in my days as a professional taxidermist and the zillions of others recounted to me as a newspaperman only a handful were taken by hunters who studied, schemed and outwitted that particular animal. Most big bucks simply fall prey to fate rather than a hunter's guile. Almost always the story was "All I saw was horns—never saw him before"—not "I've been watching and patterning this big boy for three years."

In the real world success in deer hunting doesn't depend nearly so much on one's ability as a hunter as it does his or her reaction to opportunity. There are enough deer to provide the opportunity; success depends on retaining composure and shooting straight.

Thus WHITETALES isn't a "secret" formula to lead you to that Boone & Crockett monster of your dreams. In fact, WHITETALES pokes some holes in some of those gimmicks and myths—you'll find statements, facts and observations in WHITETALES that you will never see in industry magazines. There are many "old wive's tales" and techniques of questionable worth perpetuated by magazine writers and editors out of ignorance or support of manufacturers whose advertising sustains the industry. It's a business gang—again, my chosen business. Just remember that it's all provided for a little education and a lot of entertainment. Magazines are useful, not gospel. In WHITETALES you'll find documented truth behind several facets of whitetails and hunting that are covered up or ignored by magazine writers and explanations of certain aspects that are pure inventions .

But don't get the idea that WHITETALES is an expose. It's more a labor of love. Deer hunting is a passion for me. Opening day for me is like Christmas for a kid—a feeling that I'm sure many of you share. I consider myself extremely fortunate to be able to sample deer hunting in many areas as means of gainful employment.

In WHITETAILS you won't find page after page of photos of me with defunct trophy bucks. Although I am considered to be very successful, I am deer hunter—not a trophy hunter—and don't claim to be an all-knowing expert on whitetails. But as a reporter I've had the opportunity to hunt with and interview true experts. WHITE-TALES is a reflection of my experiences, feelings and what I've learned from those associations.

You can thus expect plenty of solid, documented information here on the white-tailed deer and on hunting. What you won't find is the chest-thumping, tunnel-visioned rhetoric where personal observation is presented as fact—a trait common to books written by self-proclaimed "experts".

This book is written for the intermediate deer hunter. It's assumed that anyone reading this already knows the basics of deer hunting, such as shot placement, the phenomenon of antler growth, skinning, field dressing and the fundamentals of weaponry for the deer woods. WHITETALES is designed to take you a step further.

TABLE OF CONTENTS

Part V: THE HUNTERS' TOOLS

Part VI: ISSUES INVOLVED IN DEER HUNTING

Part VII: HOW-TO

Part VIII: THE BOUNTY

Part IX: IN CONCLUSION

"... the hunter perceives his prey with affection, respect and, at times, even reverence ..."
—*Stephen Kellert*

PART I:

PHILOSOPHY OF THE HUNT

"*Camp, for me, is not an escape. Life is not overly stressful and I'm not fleeing any heavy psychological loads. I have, afterall, a loving spouse and daughter whose company I truly enjoy, and who appreciate—even though they don't pretend to understand—my attraction to a living situation that civilized people consider appalling.*"

Chapter 1
Ode to a Hunting Shack:
An inspection of what makes us hunt

Let's face it; it's a shack. The roof has been patched to keep the outside out but the floor doesn't have a flat spot in it. And the water-stained ceiling speaks more of blight than of character.

The place looks lived-in even when nobody has been doing so.

Despite its sorry state no amount of insurance could ever sufficiently cover what this particular shack, in this particular place, is worth to me.

It would doubtless take extensive study by minds far more developed than this one to determine what it is that makes a hunting camp so appealing.

Noted outdoor writer John Madson best explained the feeling an excerpt from his oft-quoted "Palace in the Popple":

> . . . *No where on earth is fire so warm*
> *Nor coffee so infernal*
> *Nor whiskers so stiff, jokes so rich*
> *Nor hope blooming so eternal*
> *A man can live for a solid week*
> *In the same old underbritches*
> *And walk like a man and spit where he wants*
> *And scratch where it itches.*
> *I tell you, boys, there's no place else*
> *Where I'd rather be in fall . . .*

That says a lot. I only know how much I look forward to the short time spent in this spartan deep-woods shack each fall.

Anyone who has spent much time in the communal environs of team sports understands camaraderie and the abiding sense of sharing, teamwork and manhood.

But I have to admit that I treasure even more the days and nights after those with less dedication or free time have departed and I'm again alone with the cabin, the woods and nature. This place offers a spiritual renewal that no man ever got hanging around a saloon or behind a cluttered desk.

Sitting on the woodpile on a clear November night, sipping coffee and watching a young moon peek through the starry treetops, soaking in the varied sounds of the sleeping woodlot—these are moments to be treasured and sought again.

Camp, for me, is not an escape. Life is not overly stressful and I'm not fleeing any heavy psychological loads. I have, afterall, a loving spouse and daughter whose company I truly enjoy, and who appreciate—even though they don't pretend to understand—my attraction to a living situation that civilized people consider appalling.

Others' suggestions of adding electricity, running water and indoor plumbing are quickly discouraged. Furry intruders, a grown-over access road and a breezy outdoor privy only add to the appeal of a place already blessed by the absence of telephone and television.

The author-guide with client Dr. Robert Barreca of Charlottesville, Va.

Such a place is as appalling to some as it is appealing to others. Philosophers tell us that at least part of the appeal is in living in proximity to the animals we pursue.

But I'm not sure that explains it all. We're talking a primal urge with roots too deep to be readily pulled up and examined. It's something our red-skinned forefathers recognized but that was discarded when Americans started wearing clothes.

Maybe it's just that my values are not of this century. Those of us who are different; who don't tolerate the status quo, are not necessarily wrong. The personal feeling is that we should all respect others' opinions and habits and ask only the same in return.

The desire to experience that extraordinary oneness with nature is buried deeper in some humans than others. I've turned down job offers and choice assignments that would have kept me from deer camp. But my brothers, who grew up under the same influence and guidance, choose not to hunt.

I don't pretend to know or care what causes the feeling, but I'm already looking forward to the next time.

It occurs to me, as I perch atop the aforementioned woodpile, that the reasons I hunt are important only to me; intimate reasons I'm unable or reluctant to fully share. I may not even be qualified to speak for myself. The reasons are still not complete and understood. While I don't mind sharing them with you they are probably of little value to anyone else—just as I would not try to understand your motivations based on my own experience.

Hunters in general like to paint themselves as managers of the herd, keeping species from overcrowding and dying of disease and malnutrition. It's popular to proclaim one's self an angel of mercy in the autumn woods, thwarting nature's bitchy ways with a hail of lead.

But truthfully, how many of us believe that? How many of us think of ourselves as humanitarians when they take a game animal in their sights?

I can't pretend to think that way.

To my way of thinking hunting, properly conducted, is a near-spiritual experience that makes a man feel a tranquil oneness with nature that no other human enterprise can engender. Hunting makes me feel that I am once again part of the great scheme that brought us here and that orders the style of our passage through this small slice of history.

The hunter "feels tied through the earth to the animal he pursues."

Ortega y Gasset in his classic treatise on hunting, put it in a way I'll never forget:

"When one is hunting, the air has another, more exquisite feel as it glides over the skin or enters the lungs; the rocks acquire a more expessive physiognomy, and the vegetation becomes loaded with meaning. All this is due to the fact that the hunter, while he advances or waits crouching, feels tied through the earth to the animal he pursues."

Environmentalist Stephen Kellert, whose categorizing of hunters and anti-hunters is detailed in Chapter 7, expanded on Gasset's view by noting that "... the hunter perceives his prey with affection, respect, and at times, even reverence." He is therefore confronted with "the paradox of inflicting violence" on a world he admires and cherishes. He alone is compelled to rationalize the death of the animal.

When confronted by articulate opponents pointing an accusing finger at the morality of killing I'm not ready to simply concede that we are helpless as human carnivores, damned to kill. But rather, as Paul Shepard noted in his "Theory on the Value of Hunting": "... that the superb human mind operates in subtle ways in a search for an equilibrium between the polarities of nature and God. To share in life is to traffic of energy and materials the ultimate origin of which is a mystery, but which has its immediate source in the bodies of plants and other animals. As a society, we may be in danger of losing sight of this fact. It is kept most vividly before us in hunting."

I understand, appreciate and maybe even envy both the feelings expressed the eloquent manner in which they were presented by these philosophic types.

But still it angers me that we are forced to defend something that has been deemed honorable since the beginning of recorded time. When you consider the prodigious time span of intensive human hunting in North America, it takes quite a reach of imagination to regard hunting as "unnatural" or as alien to our continent.

You've been privileged if you've ever spent any time among the last of the native North American peoples—the Inuits and their like living in the northern barrens. They are the last of our continent to still literally hunt for their supper. The uninitated should note that these people no longer have to hunt. They continue by choice. They don't hunt to live but rather live to hunt. One can't help but notice how much they love the outdoors, or the importance they place on hunting as a social activity and its value as an expression of skill and knowledge. Successful hunters are afforded prestige among these native people. Hunting is important because of the freedom and self-sufficiency inherent in a hunting lifestyle.

All but the most virulent of anti-hunters condone the subsistence hunting of natives. The antis view natives' hunting as a necessity; not recreation. Yet these native people hunt with a passion. To them, in fact, pleasure is among the deepest and most vital rewards of hunting. I submit that in our own culture motivations for hunting are multiple and complex, including a range of economic, social and personal dimensions.

This pretty much underscores the veracity of making ethical judgements about hunting based on motivation. You are reminded that some fundamental Christian denominations judge sexual activity motivated for pleasure as immoral—yet find moral the same act performed in the name of procreation.

C'mon now. Even those entirely devoted to a reproductive goal can often find some twinge of enjoyment in the act, not to mention emotional and psychological gratifications. Sex is another biological function, like the quest for food, involving numerous motivations that cannot reasonably be separated one from the other.

Why do I hunt? Why do I prefer to take my meat rather than have it rendered, painlessly, between Styrofoam and cellophane?

Why does a woman sew a quilt or knit a sweater when they are readily available in stores? Why does a man build his own log house or cut his own fire wood rather than rely on contractors to provide same? Why do we grow gardens when the supermarket has all we need?

The answers are many. All are correct to the one who answers.

We'll never be able to fully explain the affection for the hunt any more than we can explain emotion.

ED ASWAD PHOTO

Chapter 2

What Makes Us Different?

Virtually all of us are low enough to get murderous with flies and mosquitoes, but far fewer would pull the trigger on a deer or rabbit.

That ironic human quirk is the rule rather than the exception. Champion humanitarian Dr. Albert Schweitzer professed aversion to killing in any form. Yet his memoirs show that the same man who kept his windows closed on stifling jungle evenings to protect curious moths from the lethality of his lamp flame also used a shotgun to vanquish raptors and snakes.

While we all live in the same glass house, there are plenty of people willing to throw bricks at those of us who enjoy hunting.

You will find that those opposed to killing wildlife often draw the line according to the temperature of the creature's blood. Criteria for empathy, it seems, is the threshold of pain.

A fish dying slowly on the end of a hook and line is somehow less offensive than a buck being dispatched with a well-placed bullet. Fishing, although every bit as murderous an endeavor as hunting, is universally regarded as a mellow, relaxing recreation suitable for everyone, including children.

I know sincere people who have become vegetarians to protest the killing of meat animals—but who regularly sit down to fish dinners, or worse yet, omelettes.

It is all a matter of viewpoint, which is in turn formulated by what one is exposed to and thus impressed by.

"It's all a matter of where we draw the line, isn't it?" says Wayne Pacelle, head of the anti-hunting Humane Society of the United States and former chairmen of the Friends of Animals.

Walt Disney is the patron saint of the anti-hunting faction—a radical, generally urban block often made up of people with a big dog on a short leash in a small apartment. They tend to have less compassion for a species than for an individual animal.

The Bambi and bunny group derives its knowledge of nature from the media, not experience. Their feelings are based on misconceptions and misguided sentiment.

If you will allow for obvious overlaps and subsequent gray areas, the opposing factions can generally be predicted by their sociological backgrounds.

Urban liberal societies are used to the centralized authority of white collar bureaucrats, conveniences to shield them from nature, and meat rendered painlessly between cellophane and cardboard.

To the rural conservative, however, less government is better, the frontiersman was a hero rather than a misfit, life is a constant competition with nature and meat is rendered by blade and/or bullet.

Ask a city kid where water comes from and he'll show you the faucet. The rural child knows the source and thus the value of water. Dirt to an urban dweller is something to be avoided; to the rural type it is a valuable and life-sustaining commodity.

What the urban child learns about sex from his or her street pals is viewed much earlier by the rural child as a beautiful and warm function of life.

The urban society's connection with death is street violence and war. Animals are associated with domesticated pets rather than a source of food. These people view nature as an idyllic pastoral stage where no animal ever dies except at the hands of a cruel and inept hunter.

The rural view is more literal. There is a realization that life and death are the stock and trade of nature. If there is no mass production and mass slaughter, the whole system goes to pot.

Rural society realizes that it is only a biased human notion that death is the worst possible alternative. In the wild, it is not a matter of IF an animal will be killed but rather WHEN it will be killed.

We'll never be able to fully explain the affection for the hunt any more than we can describe emotion. Hunting's roots are simply too deep in the human psyche to be pulled up and examined.

When man assumed the role as the ultimate predator and steward, it was the sportsman who shouldered the subsequent responsibilities.

Chapter 3
Sportsmen Foot the Bill for Wildlife

The "natural order of things" is actually a situation of constant turmoil. Nature's balance is in a continual state of upheaval and it's always been that way.

We know that even in the dimness of pre-history various species came and went routinely with the ever-changing environment. When a species no longer contributes or can't adapt, Mother Nature simply trims the roster. Survival of the fittest is just that; a species either shapes up or gets shipped out.

Where climatic and geological disturbances effected the survival and evolution of specific species in past eons, today man is the determining factor.

Until late in the 19th century animals and birds were killed in prodigious numbers for meat, skins and feathers. Habitat was disturbed and destroyed to make room for man and his accoutrements with little or no concern for the original inhabitants.

We're currently destroying thousands of acres of wildlife habitat each day. Wetlands become shopping plazas, drive-in movies and trailer parks; woodlots and brushy hedgerows are cleared for housing projects, highways and fast-food outlets. Fields and rivers that escape physical destruction are ruined by the dumping of man's waste.

The large predators that once ruled over nature's delicate system of checks and balances with cruel efficiency were tantalized by the easy pickings posed by settlers' livestock and pets. To protect his interests, man eliminated the threat. And, by doing so, he assumed the responsibility as the ultimate predator—a vital cog nature's great machine.

Man's ever-active sledgehammer has undeniably knocked nature's system out of whack. And today there are those who would enthusiastically add sport hunting to the factors contributing to this gross injustice to wildlife.

The sport hunter is, however, the savior rather than the scourge of American wildlife. He has funded the incredible success story. Money obtained through the sale of hunting and fishing licenses and taxes on outdoor equipment provides an average of 77 percent of each state's wildlife agency funding, according to figures from the U.S. Department of the Interior.

Consider that from 1885 to 1910 America's big game populations dropped 80 percent. By 1897 there were virtually no white-tailed deer in Pennsylvania and less than a half million nationally. U.S. Department of the Interior's Bureau of Sport Fishing and Hunting show today's population at about 23,000,000, with close to one million living in the Keystone State.

The wild turkey was virtually extinct in its eastern range by the 1880s. Today there are huntable populations of turkeys in 49 states—including seven states in which the bird was not indigenous.

Similar stories involve Rocky Mountain elk (40,000 in 1900, about 600,000 today), the pronghorn antelope (12,000 in 1930 and 1,000,000 today), the Canada goose (from 600,000 to 2.6 million in 50 years), the ringnecked pheasant, the woodduck and native brook trout.

Endangered or threatened species, pushed to the brink of extinction by humanity per se—not by sport hunters—are being protected and rejuvenated by sportsmen's dollars across the country.

Whether wildlife species are being saved for posterity or for sport, out of guilt or genuine concern, are polemic issues that will never be answered to the satisfaction of either side.

The fact is, however, that they thrive today because of programs funded almost entirely by hunters and fishermen.

Federal programs established under the Pittman-Robertson Act of 1937, the Dingell-Johnson Act of 1950 and the Wallop-Breaux Amendment of 1984 (see Chapter 8) provide nearly $400 million for state fish and wildlife restoration each year.

Add to that the $500 million hunters and fishermen pay annually for state licenses, permits, tags and stamps, plus untold millions from the federal waterfowl stamp program and the tireless efforts of conservation groups such as Ducks Unlimited, Trout Unlimited, The National Wild Turkey Federation, the Ruffed Grouse Society, Pheasants Forever, etc.

The spin-off to non-game species is inevitable. Trees felled to improve turkey and deer habitat also benefit innumerable songbirds, small animals and insects. Habitat improved for waterfowl harbors countless species of birds, mammals, fish, mollusks and positively affects water quality, flood control, storm damage and recreational opportunities. There are 1,150 species of vetebrates in North America and all benefit from sportsmen's input—not just the less than 140 that are hunted.

When man assumed the role as the ultimate predator it was the sportsman who shouldered the subsequent responsibilities.

One must realize that everything is here for a purpose and the constant recycling is essential to the fragile balance of nature.

Chapter 4
Death: A Misunderstood Fact of Life

Just what is it in the human makeup that makes us different? What makes one person a hunter and another disinterested or even opposed? What are the primal urges that stimulate one person and disgust another?

Certainly education and environment affects the varied stances. Some people cite the difference between rural and urban mentalities. Others feel it's a subliminal feeling of kinship to pioneer ancestors.

Virtually every hunter has been asked to define his or her reasoning at one time or another. A few mumbled phrases about killing wild animals to keep others from starving are obligatory, but truthfully who really thinks that way? How many of us are afield for the express purpose of herd management?

Philosophers and psychologists can give us educated opinions on what makes us hunt. But I'm not convinced anyone knows the answer. I suspect the true reasoning is too complex; still a dark area in our still-evolving knowledge of the human psyche.

At any rate, the reality of killing something weighs heavily on any mentally balanced, God-fearing conscience. And there can be no argument that hunting is wanton killing.

But, when you think about it, all life revolves around death. Life and death are the stock and trade of nature. It is a quintessentially human notion that death is the worst of all natural events. Such a view blindly ignores the adaptive role of early death in most animal populations.

Nature kills as a routine and essential element in survival. Death is a fact of life. Without wholesale death and reproduction, the whole system would head south in a handbasket.

I was fortunate that those questions were answered for me early in life. The education came one sunny Saturday when Dad was helping to build a tractor shed on an uncle's farm and reluctantly agreed to take me along.

Watching sheds being built is boring stuff. It doesn't take long for a 5-year-old mind to wander and the feet generally follow. Living in a downtown apartment (previous to our move to dairy country) hadn't afforded much chance to see cows close-up very often, so I seized the opportunity in a nearby pasture.

When the shed-builders broke for lunch, I towed Dad to the pasture to see the sad-eyed calf that I'd been studying much of the morning. Since fathers know everything, I pumped him for answers.

It was fine to discover that there are daddy cows and mommy cows and baby cows. And that cows are on earth to give milk. But the Gospel according to Walt Disney that I'd absorbed regularly in those early years left me totally unprepared for Dad's explanation of cows' other uses.

The thought of that fluffy, awkward, big-eyed calf being transformed into Big Macs, dog food and shoe leather was enough to blow a kindergartner's mind.

But the patient and thoughtful explanation that followed will stay with me forever. Dad is gone, but those few tender moments in the remote corner of that pasture are part of his legacy. I learned that day that there are certain organisms placed on earth for the sole purpose of dying so that other organisms can live.

Prey animals are here only so that predators can live, he said. A 2-year-old wild bird or small mammal is a rarity; 3-year-olds virtually nonexistent. Livestock's sole purpose is for human use.

Humans have killed off the predators and used wildlife's homes, he explained, which means that we have to assume the roles of the predators.

Everything has its purpose; death isn't necessarily bad. In fact, Dad explained, death is good if it's not wasted. Even people get recycled, he pointed out.

I grew to see hunting as far less brutal than sledge-hammering a tethered bull in a slaughterhouse. Or boiling a live pig or lobster. If you saw how chickens were killed and processed, McNuggets would be stricken from your vocabulary, not to mention menu. Veal and lamb would take on a whole different meaning if you ever saw how the infant animals are reared in tight boxes to keep them from walking and firming their muscles before butchering time.

One seldom hears anyone speak out against fishing or butterfly catching, but each culminates in a brutal death. How about those white rats that we inject with cancer cells and saccharin?

Who cries out when you squash a mosquito or eat an apple or kill the crabgrass in your lawn? I've yet to hear anyone speak out against the December ritual of killing an evergreen and propping up its corpse in the living room for display.

How could the act of killing any animal even approach the heinous technique of poly-ploidy—the intentional human manipulation of genes in plants and animals to mutate their growth and offspring?

One must realize that everything is here for a purpose and the constant recycling is essential to the fragile balance of nature.

I realize it because long ago a very special man took a couple of minutes to explain to a little boy how the world really works.

Thanks Dad.

How many times over the years have I dreamed of a wide-racked monarch of the forest wandering into bow range of this thicket?

Chapter 5

A Welcome Visitor

His presence is betrayed by dawn's first rays reflecting off an antler tip.

Only now can eyes fogged and swollen by lack of sleep discern the pale presence of his graying muzzle and throat patch contrasted against the sun and shadow dapple of the woodland floor.

There's no way of knowing how long he's been there, standing in the thick brush at the edge of a small clearing. He simply materialized as the young sun's rays gradually strengthened into thickening beams cutting through the forest canopy to the leafy carpet.

His attention is directed at two does alternately cavorting and browsing on the other side of the clearing. But he's not sufficiently interested to forego the security of the concealing brush. Not yet anyway.

He is drawn here by the rut. Hormonal urges temporarily cloud an otherwise cautious manner at this time of year. Maybe they will be his downfall.

He is no stranger. I've seen him five times in the last four years, but always at a distance well beyond the range of the shotgun or bow I was carrying. He is readily identifiable, carrying that long-tined 8-point rack with a deservedly regal bearing.

Antlers of his stature are crowns hereabouts, where forkhorns and spikes are the norms rather than exceptions. Yes, it's definitely him.

Our past meetings were always on his turf, a half-mile from here in a long gully snarled with briars and low slung conifers long unbothered by human objectives.

He is able to pass through that gully like a whiff of woodsmoke riding the thermals; melting into it to escape hunters, dogs and merciless winters. The gully is his place; his domain.

But here he is a visitor, lured by libidinal urges to trespass in this tiny thicket that has been my second home for more than three decades.

The thicket, bordered by pasture and power line, is only about 150 yards wide and maybe twice as long. It's a literal neck of woods, a natural conduit for deer, providing cover for their daily trips to a larger woodlot that serves as a bedding area.

The thicket is also less than 300 yards from my boyhood home and, despite its mundane appearance, has served as a combination paradise, frontier and learning center for me and my pubescent cronies in the 1950s and '60s.

Back in the days when we found girls uninteresting—the dark ages before the microchip revolutionized childhood—we spent an inordinate amount of time outdoors.

Deep, dark, full of bashful creatures and wild plant growth, this patch of woods was a classroom, a wonderland, a setting for our make-believe and an outlet for our exploratory urges. It was also ideally situated so as to allow quick passage back to the security of home in times of terror or hunger.

Even as I outgrew childhood, when I first realized that the sight of Marilyn Monroe made me feel funny—and later when I developed an intense interest in more corporeal ladies closer to my own age—the thicket remained a constant in my life. It was a place to sneak a cigarette or a purloined beer; to read girlie magazines; to be alone while pondering the mysteries and agonies of growing up.

Later, I trapped raccoons here. I shot my first rabbit and first squirrel here. I studied, photographed and killed deer here.

In the mid-1970s I built a treestand for photography, bowhunting and as a haven to escape the stresses of the grown-up world. It is from that perch that I now watch this antlered intruder.

This is my spot. I suffered the obligatory childhood broken arm in a fall from an apple tree less than 75 yards from this stand. It was at the base of this perch that my adventurous brother encountered a "blue gorilla" that scared the bejabbers out of him, defied mammalogical definition and became family legend.

How many times over the years have I dreamed of a wide-racked monarch of the forest wandering into bow range of this thicket. Now he is here, intent, stonelike—resisting the procreative urges that would coax him into the open to greet the does.

I know of at least three occasions when other hunters missed him at seemingly point-blank range in the last four years. Perhaps fate protected him long enough to set up this very meeting.

He's less than 25 yards away. Just one step would put him in a clear shooting lane.

One fateful step. Take it. Take it and you're mine; a dream will be fullfilled.

Maybe it's fate, or a betraying shift in the gentle breeze. Maybe it's just the innate sense that all prey animals have in the presence of a predator. Whatever. He doesn't take that step.

Instead, he quietly withdraws from the edge, ignoring the does as he melts silently into the leafy underbrush.

I'm alone again but not lonely; left with an abiding sense that the visit ended as it should have.

This is my place. I can only thank him for dropping by.

"Sweetest little wife, I think all the time of my little laughing, teasing beauty ... and I could almost cry I love you so. But I think the hunting will do me good."
                                                    —*Teddy Roosevelt*

Part II:

THE HUNTER

Why tie up a lot of money in something that may well be a passing phase?

Chapter 6

Getting Started in Hunting Without Breaking the Bank

That teen driver in your family probably thinks that a Ford Probe GT would be a nice first car.

You, meanwhile, were thinking more along the lines of a 12-year-old Chevy. Either, afterall, serves the purpose of getting them from here to there and back.

Your son's newest girl friend is into into music and he wants to take up the guitar. There's this boffo $750 Fender down at the music store, he says. Uncle Bob has a 6-string in his closet that hasn't been used since he upgraded. It's got a few scratches but is in good shape and he'll part with it for $50.

Likewise your kid has long been interested in your hunting and shooting. Now he or she is old enough to take a participatory interest. Gee dad, a custom glass-stocked, pillar-bedded .270 like yours would be great.

You'd love to share that enjoyment afield with them, but is it worth a couple of grand investment on what might be a whim?

In their words, "yeah, right." Translation: Hell no.

Today's obsession can be greeted with a wrinkled nose or shrug tomorrow. There's simply too much competition for young peoples' time and interests today. Blame it on the microchip, the cathode-ray tube, Walt Disney, MTV, new morality—it simply ain't like it used to be.

Let's face it. We're from a simpler era. I, for instance, grew up a country kid. There were chores, beckoning woods, few playmates, no playgrounds. TV wasn't popular until I neared high school and travel was restricted to foot or gearless, fenderless bicycle. It was a great way to grow up.

My daughter lives in a different world. She's had it tough. Heck, we didn't get cable TV until she was in elementary school—and went without a VCR until she was almost 9. It didn't really matter, however.

Between dance classes, music lessons, computer club, Brownies and Girl Scouts, and later video games and sports and boys, television was merely a fill-in.

Today, if a youngster even finds time to show an early interest in an outdoors endeavor such as hunting or shooting there is a good chance—indeed a distinct probability—that interest will eventually be compromised by any of a myriad of other diversions.

The common sense approach to life as a parent includes not spending top dollar on anything that stands a chance of being outgrown in terms of physical stature or attention span. Quality counts more as the growing years wane.

As an aside, it should be noted here that exposure to hunting and shooting is no longer solely a parent-child province. Statistics show that a growing number of first-time hunters and shooters are adults.

The increasing number of one-parent households, urban influence, competition for time, etc. means less and less outdoors introduction by parents. Young adults who have never experienced the outdoors are being introduced by workmates and other peers.

But for the same reasons, they don't want to spend a lot on an uncertain situation. Why risk a financial apocalypse over whether a fledgling hunter finds ecstacy or distaste with that first headshot on a squirrel or rockchuck?

There is plenty of inexpensive but very functional ordnance out there—and ways of enhancing its performance—that can serve as a foundation for beginning shooters.

Start with a reasonable gun—one that won't intimidate the novice with its heft or recoil.

Be advised that inexpensive does not mean low quality or compromised safety. Today's insurance codes don't allow that. An inexpensive version of any major manufacturers' line is usually only a difference in wood and finish.

The barrels and actions come off the same machines as the higher-priced, fancier-finished models in the same lines. A Winchester Model 70 Ranger Ladies/Youth rifle has the same action and barrel as their $1,500-plus custom shop Model 70s only with a shorter, decidedly more austere stock.

An New England Firearms Handi-Rifle ($189.95 suggested list), for instance, is a mechanical and performance twin to the $249.95 H&R Ultra Rifle.

Finish and checkering, you see, do not a shooter make. The unit is functional enough to be sold without a substantial loss if that original eagerness wanes.

We started my daughter out with an NEF Handi-Rifle in .223 that I found for $160 and an interchangeable 20-gauge barrel for $22 more. A youth stock (12.5-inch pull) was added for $20. We put one of my scopes on it and had an excellent starter system without threatening the mortgage money.

I chose the Handi-Rifle over the NEF Pardner ($69.95 at Walmart) because the former's investment cast, heat-treated receiver can be fitted for other rifle and shotgun barrels while the case-hardened Pardner receivers are less versatile.

My daughter started out with the short-stocked 20-gauge and grew into the longer stocked .223 that provided an incredible amount of pleasant shooting and hunting experience and plinking fun. She didn't take a beating and neither did dad's wallet.

In fact it was so much fun shooting together that dad sprung for a bull-barrelled .22-250 H&R Ultra Rifle that may even keep him interested in shooting for a while.

As the user gains experience and begins to demand more from the gun, there are some simple accuracy improvements that can be made to virtually any low-end new or used gun.

Understand that few guns will shoot a minute of angle right from the factory. Some will, but most won't. But given today's barrel-making technology and the availability of better steels, MOA potential is usually there.

"A trigger job would be my first move," says Adamstown, Pa., master gunsmith Mark Bansner. "You want it so that it's comfortable and predictable shooting off the bench and breaks at about three to three and a half pounds with no creep.

"A trigger job will mean more to your groups than a lot of other things we can do simply because it's a human error factor. If the trigger is lousy you're not going to shoot the gun well even if it is an accurate gun."

A trigger job, polishing the crown and making sure the barrel and action is adequately bedded will go miles toward realizing the average rifle's potential.

There are plenty of other accurizing moves that can be made, but the aforementioned three should go a long way toward getting a rifle to realize MOA potential with factory ammunition.

Always use the best possible factory loads. That will go a long way toward separating shooter error and the rifle's actual accuracy.

"One other thing is teaching the shooter to take care of the bore—how to clean it properly," Bansner said. "You can wipe many of the evils of inaccuracy right out of the barrel—and you'll never know how well that gun can shoot until it is clean."

Another tip: Use quality scope mounts and the best glass you can afford. The gun is going to take a beating from a beginner and good mounts are needed to keep it on track.

A good scope on a solid mount will reliably tell you where and how consistently that gun is shooting.

"A poor scope just adds to the confusion if you think the gun isn't shooting right," Bansner said.

Bansner is no fan of see-through mounts, which he sees a lot of due to the close-quarters hunting mentality of the Northeast. He advises the quick-detach variety if the shooter insists on a scope-or-sights option.

Regardless of equipment, it should be noted that a beginner needs a good teacher. Dad or a peer isn't always the answer—at least in the formative stages.

The Police Athletic League and many NRA-sponsored programs welcome beginners of all ages. Youngsters can also get quality instruction from local 4-H or NRA Eddie the Eagle programs. In some states the game commissions or local rod and gun clubs run clinics and classes.

With youngsters, the next step is personal—one-on-one with you and the youngster.

Here are some guidelines to help maintain interest and hopefully build a future shooting/hunting partner:

* Keep sessions and equipment simple. Make it fun—not intimidating or confusing.
* Use a reasonable gun—one that fits the shooter and won't intimidate a beginner with its heft or recoil.
* Don't shoot or hunt too seriously in the presence of kids. Nothing turns a teen off faster than a parent's actions.
* In the beginning, keep the session short. When the action is slow, or sometimes even when it's hot, kid's have a short attention span. It's always best to leave a kid wanting more than getting bored.
* Start out shooting at easy targets and hunting plentiful game. Kids want results.
* If a shooting or hunting session lags or gets tedious, be prepared to put the guns up and do something else for awhile. Take a nature walk with or without the guns; make a contest out of tree or bird identification; read the sights, sounds and wind—make it a memorable experience even if the original goals fall short.
* If you're hunting, make sure to bring a change of clothes for your little partner and have something fun to eat—lots of it.
* Absolutely observe very strict safety rules. Regardless of the fun, this is a learning experience.
* Above all, remember that this is supposed to be fun. Don't let lagging interest or childish attitudes discourage you.

The whole is idea is to foster an interest for a lifetime.

Chapter 7
Categories of the Hunter

Human nature is something far too complex for mere mortals to ever fully comprehend or diagnose, let alone explain. There are few observations on the subject that cannot be—or are not—challenged or mistrusted.

Yet, as in deer hunting, anyone who has undertaken even a limited exploration of the subject grows profound and claims to have stumbled across the ultimate truth.

Behavorial scientists, who have studied human nature more than most of us, still like to arrange humanity's multitude of gray areas into neat, concise categories.

A couple of behaviorists from the University of Wisconsin once researched that fascinating subspecies, the hunter. Predictably, they came up with neat, concise categories.

Dr. Robert Norton and Dr. Robert Jackson released their findings in the early 1980s. Their findings show that hunters can be broken down into five stages. Some experienced hunters have passed through all five while others may rise to one level and stay.

Whether or not you agree with the doctors' study, you will probably recognize yourself or someone you know in each stage.

The first is the "Shooter" stage. Hunters at this level often equate the satisfaction of the hunt with getting some shots at game. The quarry is secondary. Almost everything represents a potential target (and a test of the budding hunter's ethics). The major thrill of the hunt comes form the manipulation of the firearm or bow in an attempt to take game.

Can you imagine what Freud would do with that one?

The second of Drs. Norton and Jackson's stages is called the "Limiting Out" stage. These hunters still appeared to gain satisfaction from shooting but measured success—and themselves— through the number of birds or animals taken.

Filling a deer tag or taking the limit of ducks or rabbits was the criteria for measuring the success of a hunt or hunter. The quarry may be recognized as a game species but there are few self-imposed restrictions. Killing is important.

The "Trophy" stage comes next and marks the transition to the first level of self-imposed selection. These hunters describe satisfaction in terms of selectivity of game and are usually far more experienced and usually more serious about hunting than the previous stages.

These guys usually enter the stage as "bucks only" types, having "graduated" from meat hunting. The later Trophy Stage hunter is one who passes up the forkhorn or six-point buck on opening day with the idea that nothing less than a past-the-ears eight-point will do—even though the small-racked deer might have provided just as much meat.

Killing is important in this stage, but the restrictions may be so severe that they limit the outcome. This stage can progress, depending on the seriousness of the hunter and the opportunities he or she can afford, to a point where only "book" animals are considered worthy.

Another trait of this stage is the willingness to travel distances to hunt areas that might produce the more desirable animals.

The fourth stage is the "Method" stage, characterized by an intensity that rivals religious fervor.

Hunting to these folks has become one of the most important dimensions of life. Taking game is secondary to the method by which the game is pursued and subdued. A typical characteristic of the Method hunter is the amassing of a great deal of specialized equipment.

Using a grunt tube and rattling antlers for deer or bugling for elk might be characteristic of this stage (although those techniques are often found in other stages, also). Taking the animal on its own terms in its own environment, usually with a weapon or method that severely limits the hunter's capabilities, is all-important to the Method stage hunter. He or she usually hunts alone—often with a bow or muzzleloader—tied to the land and nature by the prey. In this stage killing becomes less important but still is a major element in the hunt.

ED ASWAD PHOTO

Equipment is important to the "Method" hunter.

The final hunter stage in the study is the "Sportsman" stage. North and Jackson describe it as a mellowing out which is seldom reached before a hunter's 40th birthday. Dr. Jackson says this is the stage where the hunter no longer hunts to kill but rather kills to hunt. Bagging game actually becomes symbolic to the Sportsman hunter.

The Sportsman finds satisfaction in the total hunting experience. He or she is fully mature as a person and as a hunter. They no longer need to measure their worth or control their world by taking game. Satisfaction is described in terms of appreciation of nature of camaraderie. They are satisfied merely to be afield—to experience the outdoors in its completeness, mixed with the anticipation of the hunt.

The taking of game is just a part of the total experience for people in this stage.

Another interesting study on the nature of the hunter was done by Stephen Kellert at Yale's School of Forestry and Environmental Studies. Sampling hunters nationwide, Kellert put them in three categories.

The first stage, called "Utilitarian/Meat Hunters", constituted the largest group (43.8 percent) in the study.

Members of the "Utilitarian/Meat Hunter" group were usually rural residents and were primarily interested in meat as bounty, harvesting it as one might walnuts, apples or mushrooms.

Hunters in this category had little interest in animals or their environment. To these guys the joy of being in the outdoors, without the possibility of "harvesting" an animal, was not appealing.

The next group, the "Nature Hunter", was the smallest (17.7 percent of those surveyed) but hunted most often and tended to be the youngest. As a group they were the most knowledgable about the animals hunted and sought to be involved with wild animals in their environs.

This group holds a deep affection for wildlife and they alone were faced with the paradox of taking the life of something they loved.

The third category was described by Kellert as "Dominionist/ Sport Hunter" and was second-largest at 38.5 percent of those surveyed who'd hunted consisently over the last five years.

The Dominionist/Sport Hunter's knowledge of wildlife was very small—the only group surveyed with a smaller knowledge of wildlife were the antihunters. Despite this the Dominionist/Sport Hunter, who most often live in urban environments, relished competing with and mastering game animals in a sporting context.

Incidentally, Kellert also categorized two types of anti-hunters in his survey. The first was the "Humanistic Anti-hunter." These folks identify emotionally with the individual prey animal. Often pet lovers, these people have Disneyesque anthropomorphic outlooks toward wildlife—applying the human outlook toward pain, fear and suffering to the animal.

One very interesting aspect of Kellert's study was that he found only 4.5 percent of antihunters surveyed objected to all forms of hunting, including hunting for food.

In both studies there are obvious overlaps and a few contradictions among the stages and not every hunter is going to follow the structured steps outlined here. But it's an interesting look at what we have become or will become.

"And God blessed them and told them 'Multiply and fill the earth and subdue it; you are masters of the fish and birds and all the animals." Genesis 1:28
—*The Living Bible*

Chapter 8

Sportsmen—the First Conservationists

The healthy and abundant populations of wildlife that thrive in North America today didn't just happen.

If Mother Nature had her way, much of it would have gone the way of the dinosaur early in this century.

But in the middle of the 19th century, when vast buffalo herds still roamed the western prairies and flocks of passenger pigeons blackened the skies, a group of far-sighted eastern sportsmen took some historic steps for which we should all be grateful. Their actions helped lay the groundwork for today's state and federally administrated game management programs.

The first major conservation move by sports hunters was probably in 1844 when a group of prominent New Yorkers formed the New York Sportsmen's Club, which was later renamed the New York Association for the Protection of Game. The organization's primary goal was to stop the sale of game killed out of season.

The strategy was to file suit against New York City restaurants and markets that sold illegal game. The organization's success in that arena, as well as its efforts to strengthen weak game laws, proved sufficiently effective to encourage other organizations in New England. By 1900, according to Lonnie Williamson of the Wildlife Management Institute, 374 protective game societies modeled after the New York Sportsmen were active in most New England states.

These groups, and the ones that followed, were born from overwhelming concern among sportsmen about the unthinking and uncontrolled killing of wildlife during the 19th and early 20th centuries.

It was around the turn of the century that many states began to set up official game commissions—usually a direct outgrowth of organized sportsmen's organizations. In fact, when the state wildlife agencies were formed officers of the sportsmen's clubs often became the agencies commissioners.

In 1852 Maine became the first state to employ (at $25 to $75 annually) salaried game wardens. Though most state agencies limited game laws to establishing closed spring seasons, Maine imposed a bag limit of three deer per season as early as 1873.

In those developmental years, hunting licenses were not required in many states and the fledgling state agencies were financed entirely by general state funds. However, in 1895 North Dakota made it mandatory for all hunters to purchase a license from the state, with funds appropriated to the game commission.

From those modest beginnings developed a network that raises and spends billions annually in support of fish and wildlife. The Federal Aid in Wildlife Restoration Program, better known as the Pittman-Robertson Act, is perhaps the most renown wildlife conservation effort of all time—and was the idea and result of sport hunters.

According to Williamson, the original suggestion for what was to become the PR program came in 1925 from a comittee appointed by the International Association of Game, Fish and Conservation Commissioners (now the International Association of Fish and Wildlife Agencies). The committee included John Burnham of the Wildlife Management Institute, T. Gilbert Pearson of the National Audubon Society, George Selover of the Izaak Walton League and David Madsen and William Adams, representing the Utah and Massachusetts fish & wildlife departments.

It was nearly a dozen years later, however, before Carl Shoemaker pushed the Pittman-Robertson idea through Congress and into the statute books. Shoemaker, also a sportsman with a penchant for double-barreled shotguns, was head of the Oregon Fish and Game Commission before coming to Washington, DC as a staffer on the newly formed Senate Wildlife Committee. Shoemaker wrote the PR bill, gained industry support, and got the measure introduced and approved by Congress in less than five months.

The program collects special excise taxes from manufacturers on all hunting and shooting equipment and redistributes the money to state wildlife agencies at a rate based on the number of hunting licenses sold by each state. In 1950 a similar program involving fishing tackle was instituted to benefit fisheries management. It was called the Dingell-Johnson Act and was expanded in the 1980s by the Wallop-Breaux Amendment.

Since its inception in 1937 the PR program has apportioned more than $3 billion to state wildlife agencies for habitat restoration work.

Each year more than 16 million hunters pay more than $345 million in license fees and 30 million fishermen chip in another $315 million. Through special excise taxes on their equipment hunters contribute $90 million annually and fishermen $140 million to funds used exclusively for fish and wildlife restoration programs.

In addition to the government-funded programs, sportsmen also founded independent conservation groups to fund wildlife management.

The Boone & Crockett Club was among the first national groups to form, according to Williamson. That was in 1887 and was in response to market hunting and subsistence hunting by entrepreneurs and settlers that decimated big game in the Dakotas. Returning east from a two-year ranching stint in North Dakota, Theodore Roosevelt eased the pain of the carnage that he witnessed by forming the B&C Club from sportsmen who doubled as the nation's leading explorers, writers, military leaders, scientists and politicians.

Among the club's first accomplishments was getting a full troop of the Sixth U.S. Cavalry assigned to help Superintendent George Anderson control poaching and vandalism in Yellowstone National Park.

The League of American Sportsmen was organized in 1898 by George Oliver Shields, editor of Recreation Magazine. This organization, along with the Audubon Societies, the B&C Club and state game protective associations, helped enact the Lacy Act of 1900, which was the first major law affecting fish and wildlife. In essence, the act prohibits interstate shipment of illegally taken wildlife. That law eventually helped eliminate much of the market hunting for plume birds and big game.

The American sportsmen's drive to fund conservation has not been without its snags, however, according to Williamson. Take, for example, the 1911 offer by Winchester Repeating Arms to give the New York Zoological Society $25,000 annually if the society would launch a program to protect game populations. Society head William Hornaday, a vocal opponent of sport hunting and sporting arms, refused.

Winchester then approached the National Audubon Society (which was formed by noted sportsman George Bird Grinnell in 1886) with the same offer made to Hornaday. The Audubon Society originally accepted, agreeing to expand its program to check the relentless slaughter of game birds and animals. The $25,000 would have about doubled Audubon's annual income. But charges surfaced in the news media that Audubon had "sold out to the gun people who wanted to kill all the birds in the country." Consequently the Audubon board reversed itself and refused the industry's grant.

In addition to the funds raised by hunters' license and permit fees, consider the $16 million raised each year by the federal duck stamp program, the $600 million raised and spent by Ducks Unlimited since 1937 and the estimated $300,000 annually spent by sportsmen developing habitat on privately owned lands.

Without the programs engendered by those far-sighted New Yorkers nearly 150 years ago, the white-tailed deer, wild turkey, elk, pronghorn antelope, Canada goose, woodduck, trumpeter swan and brook trout would undoubtedly be extinct today.

"How does one rate the value of sport?... Babes do not tremble when they are shown a golf ball, but I should not like to own the boy whose hair does not lift his hat when he sees his first deer." —Aldo Leopold

PART III

THE ANIMAL

"Standoff"

Chapter 9

World of the Whitetail

Family: Cervidae. Genus: Odocoileus. Species: virginianus. That's the white-tailed deer in scientific terms. But it's much too general. We've all heard footloose experts from another area of the country trying to gain credibility in our backyards: "A whitetail is a whitetail, regardless of what area it's from."

The Wildlife Management Institute's comprehensive work "White-Tailed Deer Ecology and Management" (Stackpole 1984) tells us there are 38 sub-species of the whitetail with a natural range extending from the tree line in Canada at 60 degrees north latitude to sub-equatorial South America (15 degrees south latitude).

Well, yes, the gestation period of the whitetail doe is between 90 and 105 days regardless of its range. And yes, their reproductive cycle and antler growth is triggered by photoperiodism (the changing amount of light coming through the eye as days change in length with season). And yes, the bucks do lose their antlers annually and grow them again, regardless of range or subspecies.

On the other hand, while they may all be the same animal, they sure vary by location. For instance, a whitetail in Saskatchewan or Alberta (Odocoileus virginianus dakotensis or Odocoileus virginianus borealis) can often weigh up to 350 pounds on the hoof and stand 40 inches tall at the shoulder. The same animal in the Florida Keys or Isla de Coiba in the Gulf of Panama (Odocoileus virginianus clavium) tops out at 50 pounds and 24 inches tall.

Something called Bergman's Rule notes that in widely dispersed species body size is larger in relation to the individual animal's distance from the equator. The timing of their reproductive cycles, ordered as it is by the amount of daily sunlight, obviously also

varies wildly from the equator to the tundra.

And the oft-repeated belief that cold weather triggers the rut is as difficult to kill as it is difficult to believe. "General deer activity speeds up in colder weather—they're simply moving around more," says wildlife biologist Mike Hall. "But it has nothing to do with the rut. More guys are out then and they see more deer moving so they think it's the start of the rut. Do they honestly believe that something as essential to the species as the breeding season would rely on weather patterns?"

We know that the animal is incredibly adaptable, changing its habits and needs to survive and prosper around ever-expanding human habitat. We also know, however, that the northern whitetail needed some help from Man. All but extirpated from much of its northeastern range by the turn of the century due to market hunting and habitat destruction, whitetails returned to flourish thanks to conservation measures established by sportsmen (see Chapter 8).

As an example the species was all but wiped out by 1900 in Pennsylvania but today more than 1 million whitetails roam the Keystone State.

One graphic sign of man's and whitetails' tug-of-war over habitat is carcass of a car-killed deer. A recent study showed that as many as 120,000 deer are killed annually by vehicles in New York and Pennsylvania alone.

The great northern whitetail (Odocoileus virginianus borealis), like the ones that bore these racks in New Brunswick, often reach body weights of more than 350 pounds.

But another whitetail subspecies (Odocoileus virginianus cla-vium) living in the Florida Keys seldom tops 50 pounds in body weight.

We also know that behavior varies substantially with location, according to research done by Larry Marchinton of the University of Georgia and David Hirth of the Unversity of Vermont. Take range, for example. Many eastern whitetails have a core range of about a mile. Food is plentiful in these agricultural areas. So is company.

But ranges differ in size according to various environmental factors and individual characteristics. Climate directly affects deer range. In the more northern climates the whitetail's home range tends to be larger and less stable than in the south. In midwestern states such as Wisconsin, Minnesota and South Dakota, however, the deer home range, including seasonal changes, averages about 11.8 miles.

Home-range size for whitetails often decreases as population increases. And in areas where climate has a major effect, whitetails often migrate with traditional routes ranging from 4–5 miles in parts of Minnesota to nearly 34 miles in areas of South Dakota and Michigan's Upper Peninsula.

We also know now that whitetails can see certain colors—a total departure from the long-held belief that they lived in a world of black, white and shades. Studies at the University of Georgia found that whitetails see relatively well in all areas of the color spectrum except red and see very well in the blue sector—much better than humans, in fact. That could explain early color researchers' observations that hunters in blue jeans spooked deer more quickly than those wearing orange.

In part of the research a human with a color vision deficiency believed to be identical to deer vision could detect some configuration of a fluorescent orange-clad model but found it much easier to see in some fabrics than others. He could not, however, detect fluorescent orange in a camouflage pattern.

We also know that deer communicate by spreading secretions from glands on their foreheads, tear ducts, legs and between their toes, but that many of the signal scents left by those secretions have an extremely short life—a matter of less than an hour.

Studies at Clemson University have found that scrapes are a veritable social bulletin board used by many animals. Studies at Auburn University showed that 90 percent of all activity around a scrape was done in daylight hours while 95 percent of all rubs were made at night. The same study also found that age of the animal effects scrape activity (young animals make more rubs and scrapes) as does the buck-doe ratio. A high percentage of does retards scrape activity "because there isn't as much need to advertise," according to researcher Keith Causey.

Causey also noted that the studies showed that the size of a tree rubbed had nothing to do with the size of the buck that made the rub. In fact, he said, many bucks used the same rub.

Yes, we know a lot about the whitetail. Afterall, they're virtually everywhere in the American habitat. But we always want to know more.

Readers often marvel at how wildlife photographers can get close enough to a big buck in the woods to get those well-lit, close-up shots used on magazine covers and calendars. Afterall big bucks like those are usually nocturnal and very seldom venture forth in bright light.

CHARLES ALSHEIMER PHOTO

The simple truth is that virtually no wildlife photographer shoots pictures of animals in the wild. Most photography is done in parks or preserves where the animals are not hunted and thus have no fear of humans. They also are fed better and grow older, which makes for bigger racks and better photos.

Chapter 10
Should We be Culling Spikes?

The shot rang out about 100 yards ahead of me. Since I'd made this particular drive before, I knew who was posted in that area.

"Over here, Dave," Van's distinctive gravely voice served as a locator in the thick brush.

Stepping through the briars I could see the old hunter, his body bent by age and infirmity, standing over a fallen deer.

"Just a damned spike," Van said, punctuating the statement with a spit of tobacco juice, the remnants of which darkened the familiar stain on his always-stubbled chin. "Meat; that's all. Just like the runt in a litter of puppies. Don't amount to much and never would have."

For the next 10 minutes the old hunter, racked with emphysema and arthritis in what would be his last season afield, explained the facts of life to the neophyte before him. The facts of life as they pertained to spike bucks, that is.

"If you're gonna be a buck hunter you'd best shoot every one of these guys you see. Get rid of them before they can breed—don't want ponies breeding your best mare."

The lesson done, Van leaned his timeworn shotgun against a tree and reached feebly for his belt.

"Damn. Musta left my knife in the truck. Why don't you dress him out while I go hunt us up some help for the draggin'. . . ."

The scene took place nearly 30 years ago and served as part of my education as a deer hunter. Lord only knows how often similar scenarios (complete with the delegation of field-dressing duties) have been repeated throughout history and across the country—the savvy veteran passing on his experience and knowledge to the next generation. In those days the word of the elders was gospel, at least in my neck of the woods. Quite often lessons learned in the

field were backed up in the myriad magazine stories and books that I poured over with far more enthusiasm than was expended on school work.

In effect, they were my textbooks for Deer Hunting 101. Today they're referred to as "professional journals" in IRS terms.

The adage of culling spikes for the sake of the herd was borne out virtually everywhere in print.

"The bottom line is that spike bucks are really inferior animals of inferior lineage, and that they will never grow up to sport the kind of trophy racks that make whitetail bucks the most beautiful animals in the world." Those weren't Van's words but rather those of famed whitetail photographer Erwin Bauer in his 1983 book "Deer in Their World".

A landmark study started in 1973 at the state-run Kerr Wildlife Research Center in Kerrville, Texas, served only to confirm that some spikes would always be spikes, regardless of nutrition. The study also showed that those spikes could pass their genetic have-not status onto the herd, if allowed.

Consider, however, that the study of whitetail deer is a relatively new concept. It's rare to find any professional papers written on the subject prior to the 1960s. Thus, as an emerging science, theories in whitetail biology are constantly being challenged and changed. The Kerrville study ran from 1973 through 1989 and only recently has come under the microscope of further investigation.

Many questions have come up in recent years and the adage of "once a spike, always a spike" is now thought to be inaccurate. The latest theory is that the culling of spikes may not only be ineffective but may also be damaging to the herd's gene pool.

Dr. Harry Jacobson, head of genetics research at Mississippi State University, has raised more than 200 whitetails at his research complex in Starkville and concludes that spike yearlings might be just as likely to eventually grow Boone & Crockett quality racks or to sire offspring that grow B&C racks, as fork-antlered yearlings are.

Dr. Jacobson does not recommend selective culling of spikes. He cites several B&C class bucks at Starkville that were spikes as yearlings and a 235-plus point non-typical that wore a small fork-horn and a spike as its first rack.

Dr. Jacobson also points out that the elimination of spike bucks in populations of high-buck harvests and low-doe harvests can actually lead to the production of MORE spikes.

Doe-buck ratios distorted in the favor of adult does result in a later rut because does waiting for an available buck may not be bred until their second, third or even fourth estrous cycle (24 hours every 28-30 days). The resultant later fawn birth translates into younger yearlings that are almost invariably spikes after 18 months.

Naturalist Leonard Lee Rue III, the world's most published outdoor photographer and an internationally known expert on whitetailed deer, points out the Kerrville study is flawed. Rue notes that for decades Texans were legally forbidden to shoot spikes, artificially creating a breeding pool of genetically inferior deer that would compromise any findings.

A 3.5- or 4.5-year old spike there would be larger and stronger than a younger multi-tined buck and would dominate in breeding exchanges. In a dominance fight a buck with long spikes could easily slip inside a wider rack and inflict more pain and damage.

Rue also questioned if inferior genes or malnourishment were bigger factors in the stunting of the Kerrville herd. "Data from that Texas study has been misinterpreted by hunters and writers," said Auburn University researcher Keith Causey. "All it really showed was that it is possible to select (breed) for smaller-bodied deer."

Biologist Al Brothers livetrapped a buck fawn on the Edwards Plateau in Kerr County, which supports one of the densest deer populations in North America. The fawn was removed before it became skeletally stunted by the lack of nourishment and was transferred to good range in Webb County, Texas. When the buck was killed at 4.5 years old it exhibited normal body weight for that area and a good 10-point rack.

Whitetail research has also made it clear that while nutrition and age are major players in building a big rack, there is another factor that is as equally important as the size of daddy's headgear.

"The biologists that I deal with tell me that a buck's antler potential has as much to do with the mother's genes as it does with the father's," says Knight & Hale's Chuck Jones, a frequent lecturer on whitetail hunting.

Indeed it's been noted that intensive selection of males (i.e., culling), even for many generations, will not remove bad genes unless you can also identify the female carriers and selectively eliminate them. Since does carry no visible signals of their genetic quality that "selection" is virtually impossible in the wild.

Dr. James Kroll performed whitetail research at Stephen F.

Austin State University in Texas and, as a ranch manager, has probably produced more Boone & Crockett racks than any man extant. When the first Kerrville studies were published in the 1980s he supported them enthusiatically, using both seminars and print to call for the culling of yearling spikes for the betterment of any herd.

But Dr. Kroll no longer feels that way. His conversion came as the result of his initiating spike culling programs at several of his managed properties in the deep south that quickly resulted in mediocre herds.

Bo Pitman, manager of the famed White Oak Plantation hunting lodge in south-central Alabama, had the same experience.

"The prevalent train of thought when we first started in this business was to cull the spikes as inferior deer," said Pitman who manages 16,000 acres of prime whitetail habitat in Alabama's renowned Black Belt agricultural region. "For the first three years we really encouraged shooting the spikes. We was rollin' over 40 or 50 spikes a year. But I noticed that our trophy (eight or more points with a spread of at least 16 inches) buck numbers weren't going up.

"It turns out that we were killing the spikes and the trophy bucks, leaving the small sixes and small eights—bucks we now know are genetically inferior—to do the breeding."

Two years after White Oak dropped its spike-culling program the lodge's trophy buck harvest increased by 28 percent. Two years later it improved by another 28 percent.

Because the central Alabama rut doesn't peak until January or February, fawns are traditionally dropped in late August and September—giving them very little time to develop antlers or body size before the next growing cycle.

Most yearling bucks in central Alabama are only 13–14 month-old spikes when hunting season opens, compared to 18 or 19 months elsewhere in the country.

"I pull the jawbones (to age the deer) on up to 400 deer every year here at White Oak," said Pitman, a former rodeo bull rider who has emerged as one of the nation's most progressive hunting managers. "And in 10 years I've only run across one spike that more than a yearling."

White Oak now evaluates its bucks after two or three years rather than as spikes.

Research in New Jersey, Pennsylvania, New York, Ohio and Michigan shows that bucks at that latitude (which effects the timing of the rut and thus the birth of fawns) with protein diets of more than 18 percent will go from buttons at seven months to rack bucks at 19 months. Slightly less protein content results in spikes but does nothing to limit the buck's potential.

Spikes are not uncommon, even on the best of ranges. In New York's agricultural-rich Southern Tier state-run check stations annually record scores of eight-point and occasional 10- or 12-point yearlings. But spikes are common place.

A Southern Tier buck bearing antlers of less than three inches may well be an advanced buck fawn that would wear buttons in another locale. A spike with antlers of more than three inches is probably a late fawn from the year before. Biologists have determined that as many as 40 percent of the region's doe fawns are bred in their first year and younger mothers traditionally breed later than adults, making for a later fawn drop the next spring.

"Anti-hunters have pointed this out saying that the fawn breeding is done out of desperation because hunters take so many deer out of the population each year," says Mike Hall, senior wildlife biologist for New York's Department of Environmental Conservation and a lifelong whitetail fanatic.

"Biologically we know that nothing could be farther from the truth. The (fawn breeding) phenomenon isn't an act of desperation but rather a celebration. It's a sign of an extremely healthy deer herd."

Spike culling, it appears, is a classic definition of counter-productive management. The bottom line—at least for today—is that a young buck may be wearing spikes for any number of reasons and the size of his first rack may have no bearing whatsoever on his eventual trophy potential.

Chapter 11
Passing up Does—Macho and Silly

The hunter backed a little deeper into the small spruce he was using for concealment and peered closer at the movement in a small thicket 100 yards west of his stand.

He had just watched a group of six deer run full-speed into the far end of the thicket. Experience told him that the group would walk through the thicket and break across the a field toward the stand of hardwoods behind him.

The hunter was positioned between the deer and their destination. Since deer live in a matriarchial society, it stood to reason that the lead deer in the all-antlerless group would be the largest doe. That and the fact that she had the longest legs.

The group cautiously exited the thicket then burst into full gallop toward the cover of the hardwoods. Without hesitation the hunter singled out the lead deer and fired.

The story would never be considered for Outdoor Life or Sports

Afield because the animal didn't wear any fancy headgear. The hairy-chested logic of the deer hunter dictates that the only acceptable quarry is a buck with large antlers.

But this doe dressed out at around 150 pounds, meaning nearly 70 pounds of boned, lean meat. And venison from does contains less calories than that from bucks (See Chapter 33). Besides, there are those who would argue that meat—not a trophy rack—is the only justifiable reason for killing.

"Anybody can shoot a doe," sneer the cynics.

Some luckless hunters would debate that. But it is true that antlerless deer are more abundant than those with horns. In perfect habitat there are five antlerless deer (mature does, yearling does and their fawns) for every antlered (18 months or older) buck.

Certainly sheer numbers make antlerless deer less of a challenge. That's what makes the stag the symbol of the hunt. Even the most conscientious hunter cannot be expected to pass up a buck for a doe. The argument isn't there, but rather with the hunter who refuses to "lower" himself or herself to legally shooting a doe.

That mentality is actually lowering the odds of seeing large—racked bucks. If you want to see more bucks, the does must be thinned out. Doe hunting is the most efficient management tool ever devised.

"Doe shooting decimates the herd. A farmer doesn't get rid of his cows."

True, over-shooting does can be devastating to the herd. Game managers use antlerless permits to trim the herd because each adult doe taken in the hunting season reduces next spring's potential by three animals (the doe and two expected fawns).

But a responsible degree of doe shooting is absolutely essential for the health of the bucks and the herd overall. For example, each season in New York and Pennsylvania between 78 and 82 percent of the mature (antlered) bucks are killed. The male fawns therefore must be given every chance to grow up and bolster the herd. But the survival rate for fawns in the wild slightly favors does, since young bucks have a higher rate of metabolism and therefore starve easier.

If the doe population is not trimmed to give the males better odds in the competition for food, there simply will be fewer bucks. Not only do does eat forage that male fawns need to survive, but their numbers reduce the amount of forage available for adult bucks. And nutrition is a major factor in antler development.

Also, a report from a team of wildlife biologists with the Pennsylvania Game Commission shows that undernourished does from over-populated regions have far more female fawns than males—while well-nourished does tend to give birth to a preponderence of male offspring.

The ideal male-female ratio is 1:1 and the big buck harvest tips Mother Nature's scales so much that something has to be done to compensate.

Equal rights pertains to all. Today's hunter can't afford to be sexist.

COUNTING THE HERD

How do biologists know the size of the deer herd, a number on which they base the number of antlerless permits to be allocated? Aerial surveys and other one-by-one head counts are logistically impossible. Hunter reports are not reliable. The use of Oujia Boards is suspected.

Actually, most state game departments keep track of the previous year's kill with some type of system and make the next year's allocations from there.

A system that started in New York and has been adopted in most other states calls for successful hunters to mail in reports of their kills. Banking on the fact that a percentage of hunters will fail to meet that obligation, the game department dispatches biologists to man check stations, check meat processors, deer hanging in front yards, on truck fenders at restaurants, etc.

The hunter's name and other data are taken from the tag on each deer examined and checked against the list of hunters who sent in reports at the end of the season. From this comes the percentage of hunters who reported—for example if 65 percent of the names on examined tags show up in the "reported" file then the state assumes a 65 percent report rate overall and adds 35 percent to the reported kill to get the "calculated harvest."

There are certain biometric data factored into that formula, but that's basically it. In New York the system was audited by an outside agency and was found to be statistically accurate to within plus or minus 1 percent.

What seems like an obvious humanitarian act can actually be a matter of killing through kindness. Rest assured that Mother Nature knows what she's doing.

Chapter 12
Feeding Deer Can be Killing With Kindness

Conversation and breathing comes in billows of steam, making the cross-country skiers look like cartoon characters. Leaning on ski poles, they rest on the fresh trail that cuts through the snow-carpeted woodland.

The reason for the stop, aside from advancing fatigue, is a furry mound half-concealed by the fresh blanket of powdery snow. A little dusting of the area reveals the frozen body of a white-tailed fawn, emaciated and half-eaten by dogs or coyotes who serve as cogs in nature's great recycling machine.

Winter is firmly entrenched and the sight naturally turns one's thoughts to wildlife's plight in the seemingly ruthless environs.

Nothing tugs at a wildlife lover's heart more than the thought of Bambi with its ribs sticking out, struggling through brisket-deep snow. Yet it is invariably the young and weak that succumb first when times are rough.

It is a purely human notion, however, that survival of the fittest, fueled as it is by wholesale death, is anything but a marvelously efficient natural tool.

Invariably each winter someone wants to start a program to feed starving deer. Wildlife biologists and deer experts across the country offer one suggestion to those people: Don't do it.

What seems like an obvious humanitarian act can actually be a matter of killing through kindness. Rest assured that Mother Nature knows what she's doing. Virtually everything in the wildlife kingdom is balanced and human interference—regardless of intention—can have catastrophic consequences for the intended benefactor.

The herd doesn't need human help. But if you feel something must be done, cutting down trees to provide easier browse for deer in yarding areas is fine. But providing hay or commercial feed in fields or backyards can make for big problems.

When a suburban homeowner tries to feed does and fawns it seems like an act of mercy. That is until word gets around about the free lunch and the growing number of recipients turn their ravenous attention to neighbors' shrubs and fruit trees when the winter feeding stops.

One also has to consider the animals' health. The whitetail's metabolism slows by approximately one-third in winter, leaving it in a state of "walking hibernation" and thus reducing its nutritional needs. All are similarly equipped and natural selection weeds out the weakest.

Biologists from the New York State Department of Environmental Conservation, the Pennsylvania Game Commission and the Stump Sitters whitetail study group in Wisconsin offer some reasons why we shouldn't set up backyard soup kitchens for our supposedly disadvantaged wild neighbors:

* Various species of protozoa and bacteria assist deer in digesting their food. The types of bacteria are relative to the types of food eaten. A deer that changes food types too quickly risks death. Many deer that die of starvation have full stomachs but the bacteria in their stomachs was not the right type.

This apparently varies with geography. When I traveled the NRA's Great American Hunters Tour with whitetail biologist Mike Ondik of Pennsylvania, he recommended slipping winter whitetails alfalfa in extreme conditions because they could digest it easily. My traveling mate on the same Tour was Jim Zumbo, best known as the well-traveled hunting writer for "Outdoor Life". But Jim started his professional life as a wildlife biologist and said that in western states biologists warned to never feed a western whitetail alfalfa because they couldn't digest it.

* Deer quickly become dependent on their easy source of food. Once feeding begins, it must be continued on a daily basis. Interruption of the schedule can result in the elimination of all or part of the animal's diet.
* In a society of dominance such as the whitetail's, the bigger members get the larger share of the feed while the smaller, weaker members get driven away. Larger deer also often

physically batter fawns and yearlings in these situations, inflicting life-threatening injuries. Artificial feeding concentrates large numbers of deer into small areas, forcing them to become even more competitive and making them prey to disease and nervous disorders.

* Once deer become accustomed to an artificial source of food they will remain close—often ignoring more nutritional browse nearby. They'll do this even if they are receiving less than their daily feed requirements.

Another consideration, and probably the most important, is a matter of logistics. An average herd increases its population 30-40 percent when fawns are born. Not only must artificial programs continue year-to-year, but each year more food must be provided to accommodate the growing herd.

Feeding situations in New York's Adirondack Mountains have shown that sooner or later the logistics become overwhelming and can result in a massive die-off when the program can no longer accelerate in conjunction with the birth rate.

Regardless of the sentiment, it's best to let Mother Nature handle the whole affair.

"Golf is sophisticated exercise, but the love of hunting is almost a physiological characteristic. A man may not care for golf and still be human, but the man who does not like to see, hunt, photograph or otherwise outwit birds or animals is not normal." —Aldo Leopold

PART IV:

HUNTING TECHNIQUES

A white-tailed deer lives by its nose. Eating, breeding and security depend largely on the animal's sense of smell. While a whitetail may use its senses of sight and hearing a great deal, it will believe its nose above all else.

Chapter 13
Making Sense of Deer Scents

Three does venture from the dawn-lit woodlot and walk single-file across the power line clearing.

But the hunter concealed on the far side of the power line ignores them while focusing on a figure still standing in the shadows of the woodlot. He hopes that the 8-point buck he's been watching since summer is going to follow the does into the open.

The hunter arranges his rifle rest and orients the crosshairs of his scope on the area where the buck will step into the clearing behind the does. The conditions are right. The stage is set. It's almost showtime.

The does are halfway through the clearing when the leader stops. In one sudden motion she throws her tail in the air and bolts back into the woodlot from which they'd emerged. The other does quickly follow and the buck ambles off, tail down, in a slightly different direction.

Just like that a prime opportunity evaporates. The hunter was well-concealed, hadn't made a noise, and had been careful to cover his boot scent for the pre-dawn trek to his stand. So what had happened?

A film canister packed with sterile cotton makes a dandy wick to soak with deer urine and place within shooting range of your stand. When you leave simply snap the cap back on the canister and take it with you. Never leave a scent bomb. You don't want animals coming later and getting frustrated or used to it being there.

Commercial strap-on dispensers are good for covering the smell of boots and dispensing cover scent.

"At first I was dumbfounded. I'd used fox urine on my rubber boots so I was sure that they hadn't left any scent," said the hunter, John Law Jr., a veteran whitetail hunter from New York's Hudson Valley. "But as I went over the whole thing I realized something.

"I'd covered the soles of my boots with scent and splashed some on the rubber uppers. But the grass along the path was higher than my boots and those deer picked up my scent from the weeds brushing against my pant legs."

A white-tailed deer lives by its nose. Eating, breeding and security depend largely on the animal's sense of smell. While a whitetail may use its senses of sight and hearing a great deal, it will believe its nose above all else.

For instance, if a deer spots a stationary hunter, it won't bolt but rather will test the air for sound or scent to confirm its suspicion. Similarly an unfamiliar noise will put a deer on alert and activate its other senses.

But if a deer scents you the party is instantly and indisputably over. No need for visual or auditory confirmation. See ya later, no questions asked.

In order to consistently score on whitetails, a hunter has to defeat the animal's first line of defense—its nose.

"Deer research is relatively young and 50 years ago hunters had no idea how keen a deer's sense of smell was or how much it depended on that sense," said Ralph Warner, business manager for Pete Rickard Inc. of Cobleskill, NY. The company was the first manufacturer of deer lure in the early 1940s.

"Today we estimate the deer scent industry at $10–12 million (annual sales) and growing every year."

All of those products are designed to help you score in the deer woods—or at least to tip the odds in your favor. Using scent to your advantage isn't exactly rocket science, but it does take some knowledge and a little common sense.

Probably more is written about attractants than any other area of the scent game. Because of that popularity and exposure many myths and misconceptions have been spread about their use.

Food scents, for example, have long been downplayed. We've all heard the admonition that apple scent in a pine woods or acorn scent among conifers is going to alarm deer rather than attract them.

Well, that's not necessarily so. TV host and whitetail nut Peter

Biologists tell us that rubs are not only the result of a buck taking out its sexual frustration on a pliant tree but are also a means of spreading identifying scent from the deer's preorbital gland near its eye. Contrary to popular belief the size of the tree rubbed is not an accurate indicator of the size of the buck that does the rubbing.

Fiduccia, who spends more time playing with whitetails than most biologists do, once piled apples in a pine woods where there weren't any apple trees for miles. The pile drew deer almost immediately.

After the pile was depleted he used apple scent in the area and easily drew the deer to it.

Another misconception is that sexual attractants won't lure a buck except during the rut. Having watched bucks react to sexual scents in September and early October, I know that isn't true.

Penn State University essentially proved that a buck will react to sexual stimulus at any time. The University put an adult buck and doe in a large enclosure and monitored their behavior year-around. Whenever the doe was injected with the estrus hormone, regardless of the time of year, the buck would scent and mount her.

There is much controversy over sex scents. Just about all major scent companies claim to have their own deer herd, from which they extract the various type of urine used in their attractant scents. Many, however, purchase their urine in tanks from specialized deer farms.

Just about all scent companies also market a "doe-in-heat" urine that they claim is extracted only from does in their estrous cycle. Now, common sense would deem that statement dubious. Considering that a doe comes into estrous for only 24 hours and only two or three times annually if she isn't bred, that would require some very vigilant and knowledgable urine takers and an enormous herd of does to fill all the "doe-in-heat" bottles marketed every year.

Consider also that biologists who watch deer all the time can't always pick up visual clues when a doe is in heat.

A midwestern writer-TV host visited many scent companies and found no deer herds. He had most of the big-name commercial "doe-in-heat" attractants tested at a Chicago laboratory and found that none contained "pheromones" touted on the label as the magic attractant. He experimented with a captive herd and found that bucks were just as attracted to human urine as they were to bottled "sex attractants".

The result was an over-zealous expose on television and in print that resulted in his being sued by a major scent manufacturer. The manufacturer won the suit, which was designed to shut up the onslaught of writer-TV host but did not disprove his allegations.

"Mammalian urine, almost regardless of species, attracts virtually all mammals," said Auburn University researcher Keith Causey. "Urine is amazingly similar among mammals."

Many scents are made from sheep or goat urine, or mixtures with deer urine. Some biologists claim that pheromones dissipate within minutes of secretion and therefore could not be preserved in bottled urine.

Whether or not the lure was made from the urine of an estrous doe, and whether or not it contains pheromones is pretty much a moot point. Virtually every attractant scent on the market will work under the right conditions. They are probably not sexual attractants but rather signposts of an unfamiliar animal that are followed by curious bucks eager to breed or challenge other suitors.

In fact, we've been told by many "experts" that human urine will spook whitetails. But as a bowhunter and guide for Shattuck Creek Outfitters in Idaho, I've personally "freshened" too many scrapes and watched bucks attracted to them (most react angrily, as if confronted by an unwelcome stranger) to believe that human urine is anything less than an attractant.

Deer urine definitely varies due to differences in areas and individual diets. It's my feeling that regardless of his hierarchy in a herd, a buck will want to know who and how big a strange buck is. That's the attractant.

Renowned whitetail author-photographer-hunter Charlie Alsheimer of Bath, New York, uses vaginal secretions from dairy cows as an attractant for whitetails. He prefers this "white lightning" to commercial scents.

One well-known bowhunter, in fact, successfully employed his wife's used sanitary napkins as a deer lure. Bizarre perhaps; definitely a test of dedication, but effective.

How you use an attractant scent is probably more important than what type you use.

A few drops of attractant is sufficient to "freshen" an actual or man-made mock scrape. I prefer to set my stand up about 30 yards downwind of a scrape. A buck will often check a scrape from a distance downwind.

Bottles of urine carried in a hunting shirt can be messy, smelly and are easily contaminated.

"I use a film canister filled with cotton soaked with doe urine," advises Steve Lecorchick, guide and manager of Red Oak Ranch, a hunting outfitter in western Virginia. "I call them stoppers.

"You can carry them sealed in your pocket. When the time comes, I break one open and place it in such a way that when a buck lowers his head to sniff it, his head is behind a rock or tree trunk and he can't see me draw my bow.

"Just figure about three feet behind the stopper and you've got the vitals of an average buck."

Always retrieve the canister when you leave your stand. A neglected scent dispenser can draw bucks when you are not there. It doesn't take long for a buck attracted by the scent to learn there are no does there. He thereafter is likely to write off the area as unproductive regardless of the scent.

A few years ago how long a bottle of urine had been on the store shelf was a legitimate concern. Not today.

"There are so many products now and dealers are so reluctant to tie up shelf space and money that they all order just before the season," Warner said Warner of Pete Rickard's Inc. "Heat, light and temperature will effect bottled deer lure. But if it is capped tightly after use and stored in a cool, dark place it will last year-to-year."

"There have never been any definitive studies done on commercial scents' effects on whitetails," said Auburn University researcher Keith Causey. "We have never seen any reaction to commercial scents among our captive animals."

Luring a buck into shooting range is a glamor move. That's the most visual and exciting facet of using scent to score on whitetails. It must be noted here, however, that in 30 years of hunting professionally and recreationally I've never encountered a truly good hunter that used sexual attractant scents (unless he had a tie to a scent company). Every good hunter that I've ever met, however, was extremely conscious of his or her own scent and wind direction and conditions.

They weren't so interested in appealing to a deer's sense of smell as they were to avoid it.

That's where the homework comes in. You can't lure a buck without first hiding your presence from him. Obviously a hunter must first eliminate and/or cover his own scent before an attractant can be useful.

The obvious first step is to get your body clean. Body odor is strong and almost impossible to mask. Common sense dictates the use of unscented soap and deodorant. Specialty soaps are available but any unscented domestic brand is fine.

Baking soda has long been touted as an odor eater, and it does work well when an entire box is stored in an enclosed setting like a refrigerator. But it breaks down within a half-hour in open air and is therefore quite useless in a hunting setting.

Chlorophyll pills could be effective in reducing body odor if sufficient doses were taken. The catch is that the doses would have to be tremendous and are simply impractical.

Part of the body cleanup should include brushing your teeth and using baking soda as a mouth wash.

Most of these suggestions are no-brainers to most experienced hunters. Common sense pretty much covers the personal hygiene end.

But many folks overlook some obvious scent-producers. Your diet has a lot to do with the way you smell, and there is no way to mask some odors.

Take, for instance, alcohol. It can stay on your breath and its odors can seep through your pores as much as 24 hours after consumption. Many spicy food seasonings are the same. Sit next to a guy in a steam bath after a meal that included garlic, hot peppers or onions and you'll quickly see—and smell—what I mean.

In Viet Nam we had night sensing devices that could detect the difference between a meat-eating American and a southeast Asian whose diet consisted principally of rice. American Indian hunters switched to bland foods and avoided red meat for at least a week prior to a hunting trip.

If you're serious about scent control, you could do worse than to emmulate subsistence hunters to whom successful hunting meant the difference between life and death for his family rather than a rack on the wall and an occasional meal.

Your clothing is another obvious carrier of scent. Washing with and drying with unscented agents is common sense. A lot of successful hunters like to package hunting garments with natural scent producers like pine boughs or leaves. Others use a commercial earth scent.

Both are effective, but avoiding unnatural scent is just as important. Store hunting clothes away from cooking odors, smoke or other foreign odors. That also means one set of footwear for filling the car with gas and another for the woods.

Choice of footwear is absolutely essential in controlling personal scent. Rubber boots not only don't pick up or carry odors like leather boots but they also contain foot odor far better than porous leather. And, as pointed out in the opening scene, the height of the rubber boot can be a factor.

I like to use a pair of waders cut off at knee length or a high pair of black rubber barn boots with pant legs tucked in the top to keep them from touching surrounding brush.

After you've controlled your own scent, some masking scent is also needed, not only to cover any residual scent but also to create a natural illusion.

Mammal urine such as fox or coon is quite commonly used as a masking scent, as is skunk scent. I've heard warnings that grey fox urine should be avoided because greys are more aggressive than red foxes. And that skunk scent shouldn't be used because it's a skunk's alarm signal and the purpose isn't to alarm other wildlife but to calm it.

Both schools of thought are probably examples of common sense stretched out of proportion. I can only speak to the fact that I've used both grey fox urine and skunk scent successfully many times without incident.

I should also note that skunk scent applied to a pair of leather combat boots in 1979 (before I knew of rubber's preferred qualities) is still strong enough to warrant storage in the woodshed rather than in the house.

One consideration in your choice of masking scent might be hunter traffic. Jim Mason, co-owner of the Southern Sportsmen's Lodge in Hayneville, Ala., sees more than 200 deer killed on the lodge's leased land every year.

"I've switched to spraying my boots with diluted vanilla extract as a cover scent," said the renowned guide. "We have a lot hunters go through here each season and almost all of them are using fox or coon urine as a cover scent.

"I feel that the deer after a while start to equate that scent with the presence of hunters."

I prefer not to use an attractant scent to mask my own scent. Common sense says that you don't want to attract attention to yourself but rather to a spot within range of your bow or firearm.

Many hunters do, however, use attractants on their boots. The feeling is that a lovesick buck will follow the trail to your stand.

I once had that strategy backfire. I doused my boots with doe-in-heat scent just prior to leaving my truck for the trek to a bow-stand. Later a buck came into view and my excitement rose when it became evident that he was reacting to the sex scent spread by my boots.

The excitement turned quickly to frustration, however, when he stuck his nose to the ground and backtracked me out of sight. He was following the scent in the direction that it grew stronger, and since that scent wore off my boots as I walked, the odor was stronger in the direction of the truck, where I'd first applied it.

If you are going to lay down a scent trail with you boots, use a scent pad. The pad retains the scent well, keeping it strong with each step. Don't walk directly to your stand but rather in a small circle around it, or maybe in a figure-eight with your stand at the intersection. Then take off the scent pads and place them away from the stand but within range.

Pretty simple. In order to use scent to score on whitetails, first deceive the deer's nose, then appeal to it. Making sense of deer scents just takes a little common sense.

Chapter 14
Calling all Deer

To be truthful, it didn't sound like any vocalization I'd ever heard any deer make.

But the tedium of a quiet day of scouting had eroded my skepticism. Feeling that there was nothing to lose, I pulled out the Woods Wise Buck N' Doe tube call and mimicked the vocalization I'd heard on Jerry Peterson's "Vocabulary of Deer" audio tape. Jerry called it a social bleat and said it was the most common and universally effective.

Yeah, right.

Well, suddenly the leaves rustled just over the knoll. I waited two minutes and sounded the bleat again. Almost immediately a six-point buck materialized. Shows what I know.

Not expecting results, I had set up carelessly and he spotted me right away. But he didn't spook. The deer paced nervously a couple steps one way, then the other, all the while watching me.

His demeanor wasn't one of fear or curiosity. It was obvious that he considered me an obstacle—something to circumvent so that he could pursue the doe he'd just heard.

After about 20 minutes he gave up, obviously frustrated, and left the way he'd come. But one toot on the call and he returned, convinced of the mystery doe's imminence. This time it took more than a half hour before he took a wide path around my perch, grunting all the way.

It could have been a fluke. But two days later I attracted a doe and two fawns to the base of my stand with the same call after seeing them pass at 100 yards. And another morning I stopped two young deer cold with the call after spooking them on the way to my stand.

The call had the same variance of tone as a cow elk whistle,

A mouth call designed to replicate a deer's snort can be very effective for still hunters if used correctly. Deer often use a snort to acknowledge the presence of other deer.

which we find incredibly effective when guiding elk hunters in Idaho.

When I related the Woods Wise experiences in my newspaper column, every local store sold out of Woods Wise tubes the first morning. A year later I was still getting telephone inquiries on the call. Such is the mentality of the hunting public.

The view from here is that deer calls, like turkey calls, are made to attract hunters first and the animals second. Hunters will search and search for a grunt tube that sounds the way they like it.

Bo Pitman, manager of the White Oak Plantation in Tuskegee, Alabama, demonstrates the use of a grunt tube.

In point of fact, real deer grunt in so many different tones that it's foolish to say one grunt tube sounds more authentic than another. I've probably used 30 different grunts that have worked—as have a belch or two on occasion.

As a matter of fact the first deer I ever called came to inadvertent belching. Yes, Pepsi-Cola was my first grunt call.

I'd stuck a can in my daypack and pulled it out to toast the last hour of light in my bowstand. Being alone in the woods, I allowed my social graces to slip a bit and after a couple of swigs I cut loose with a loud, resonant burp.

A commercial rattling bag can be every bit as effective as actual antlers. The key is knowing when and where to rattle.

The inadvertent broadcast grunt was answered within seconds. I worked up another belch—actually two in succession—and was answered by an animal that was definitely coming my way.

It wasn't long before a basket-racked eight-point appeared and strolled toward my stand. The Pepsi grunt must have been a social note (I can't vouch for Coke or Dr. Pepper) because the buck wasn't fired up, just curious.

He was within 50 yards and in full view when I decided to grunt once again in an attempt to get him within bow range.

Wrong.

As soon as I sounded off he spotted me and bounded out of view. Probably the two biggest mistakes made by novice callers are that they call too loud and too often. Rule of thumb: If the deer is responding, stop calling.

And don't use calling in place of good woodsmanship. You've got to mind the wind and thermals, hide yourself properly and be in position to react with no detectable movement when the time comes.

TV host and whitetail nut Peter Fiduccia points out university studies from Cornell and Georgia that confirm and categorize 13 basic types of vocalizations by whitetails. Peterson characterizes at least a dozen. I've counted up to 38 variations on those.

I don't doubt the accuracy of their studies, but how important is it to master so many different calls? How important is it to use a tending grunt as opposed to a social grunt or an aggressive grunt or a hyperventilating grunt. It probably isn't as important as it is intriguing—the deer don't care as much as the hunter.

Sure, I've spooked deer away by calling, but was it the wrong word or was I simply set up wrong? Personal opinion is that it was the latter.

You see, I'm from the KISS school—Keep It Simple, Stupid. I don't like to go into the woods with more apparatus dangling around my neck than Mr. T.

Personal favorites are a good adjustable grunt-bleat call (Butski Game Calls and Adventure Game Calls make a good adjustable) and a snort (Lohman and Quaker Boy are personal favorites). Primos makes very compact Still Grunter and Still Bleat that fit in your mouth without interfering with your bowstring or gun butt. They also don't take up much room in a pocket or pack.

Timing and cadence are more important than tone or brand name. To my way of thinking most people call too loudly.

How loud is too loud? If you can only see 50 yards, don't call any louder than necessary for the deer to hear you at that distance. Their hearing is nothing short of phenomenal but varies with the conditions.

For example, the rut was in full swing and the air cold and still when Mark Lunders, a guide for Shattuck Creek Outfitters in Idaho, and client John spotted a large ten-pointer who was trying to mount a doe some 450 yards from their hilltop perch.

"The buck was persistent and the doe didn't run away, but she wouldn't stand for him," John said. "He'd browse for a few minutes, then trot over and try to mount her. Then he'd browse some more.

"We watched him for about 20 minutes. Then, when they were apart, Mark tried a soft grunt just to see what would happen. We never even figured they were close enough to hear it—but the buck reacted immediately and came right at us.

"He must have thought that Mark was another buck infringing on him. He came almost 400 yards, right to the base of the hill we were on, then hung up in the brush, grunting back at us."

The buck hung up at 80 yards, in cover just thick enough to keep Law from getting a shot with his muzzleloader—but both he and

Lunders learned something about a buck's hearing capacity.

Like turkeys, bucks will be reluctant to come uphill to a call. It's probably just a matter of limited sight range playing on their cautious nature.

Taking advantage of that caution, I've stopped at least a dozen trotting or walking deer in their tracks—and within bow or gun range—with just a quick shout or whistle. If they don't know where you are, they'll invariably stop to find out.

Each situation is different, however, and levels and types of caution can vary with the season.

Take the situation Bo Pitman, manager of the White Oak Plantation in Tuskegee, Alabama, found himself in recently. He was waterfowl hunting with his father, Robert, at a time that coincided with the downside of the deer rut in south-central Alabama.

"I saw an eight-point about 120 yards off and just grunted at him to see what he'd do," Bo said. "It was pretty thick around our duck blind, but I could tell by an occasional splash or twig breaking that he was coming to the call." It took him about 15 minutes to cover the distance and he kind of sidled right up next to the blind, looking for what was making the grunt.

"All at once a flock of ducks came to the decoys and we started shooting. I'd forgotten all about the buck. After we retrieved the ducks and got back to the blind I remembered him and grunted again.

"He was standing in the water next to the blind all that time—even while we were shooting and retrieving ducks. He just wanted to see what was grunting."

To illustrate the value of different situations, consider another anecdote. Two friends of mine were hunting the rut near the end of the New York bow season when they spotted a familiar seven-point stepping into a field about 150 yards away.

He was in full view as he browsed into the uncut buckwheat. Ken, who'd already filled his tag, grunted to the buck while Gordy got into position to shoot when the deer came their way.

But at the sound of the grunt the deer dropped into the grass and literally crawled on its stomach until it got to the edge of the field. It then leapt to its feet and bounded off into the woods.

Gordy managed to kill the buck from a treestand two days later. When he and Ken skinned the it they found that the left front shoulder was separated and there was a large puncture wound—obviously from an antler tine—under the shoulder.

The deer also had puncture wounds in its rib cage, along its nose and at the base of one eye. No wonder it wanted no part of another grunting buck.

If you're just looking to attract a deer, any deer, probably the most universally effective call on the market is the bleat. It's non-threatening and very common. Most commercial bleat calls mimic a fawn. Why would a buck or a doe other than the mother come to a fawn bleat?

Will Primos of Primos Game Calls is a firm believer that a deer will investigate anything that sounds like another deer. They are just naturally curious about the presence of another deer.

The bleat is incredibly effective year-around. I was first clued into its effectiveness when my brother-in-law, Dean Sunderland of Phoenix, Arizona, told me of the phenomenal success he'd had calling mule deer to the gun using a predator call. He blew it passively, like a fawn looking for mom, and drew mulies from incredible distances.

In addition to the aforementioned Woods Wise call, I enjoyed a great deal of success with a Quaker Boy Doe and Fawn bleater. It's nothing more than a small can that you turn over in your hand. It's long, lonesome notes have attracted deer to the bow and camera lens on a regular basis for two years.

"We use the grunt and the doe bleat a lot during the archery season," said Pitman, who manages more than 16,000 acres for whitetails and turkeys in Alabama's famed "Black Belt" deer wonderland. "That's not during the rut, when you'd think it would be most effective. But the rut comes during rifle season and you can roll an ole buck over at a couple hundred yards then, so you don't need a call.

"We use it very effectively in October to bring a buck those last few steps closer to the bowhunter."

In the last 15 years antler rattling has gone from a predominantly Texas hunting tactic to a virtually universal ploy.

If the weather, timing, herd dynamics and attitude of nearby deer are right rattling is incredibly effective. Bucks, does and fawns will congregrate to watch a good fight. Also be advised that a decent—sized buck that has recently lost a fight may shy from rattling.

It intrigues me that entire books have been written on such a narrow subject, but this is, afterall, an industry. When the word got out that I was doing an article on calls and rattling for a national magazine, more than 100 unsolicited product samples came to my door as well as scores of telephone calls from PR types I hadn't heard from in years. This is big business.

I've read that you should use only fresh antlers to get the right tone. Other guys suggest storing the antlers in water; still others seal them with linseed oil. There are published suggestions that you should saw off the brow tines to protect your hands—and elsewhere that you shouldn't take off the tines or drill carrying line holes in the antlers because it will alter the tone. I've also read that big racks are best because they give better resonance.

But just as with the commercial calls, the industry is looking to lure the hunter first and the animal second.

Not just bucks come to the sound of a fight. I was once an unsuspecting but thoroughly discouraged and frustrated witness to a half-hour fight between two small six-point bucks. That fight drew two different sets of does and fawns and a forkhorn buck from various directions.

My frustration was borne of the fact that I witnessed the whole event from 20 yards away in a treestand during archery season—after I'd squandered two arrows on misses earlier in the morning and had dropped the rest of the quiver from the stand in the considerable excitement of the two bucks' approach.

The first buck I ever rattled in came to a 25-year-old set of forkhorns I found in the corner of the garage. My next most successful set of antlers were porous, mouse-nibbled, sun-bleached mule deer sheds I found in Montana.

One particularly hot buck came to the sound of a dead maple branch rattled along the magnesium riser of my bow. I've also used $40 artificial antlers, rattling bags, etc.

The results have always been the same—if the rut was on, the buck-doe ratio right and the animal unintimidated, he would come to virtually anything that was rattled. If one or more factors of that equation were off, it didn't matter what was rattled—he wasn't coming.

Rattling bags are much easier to carry and to handle when the buck starts coming and the moment of truth nears—but by the same token there are probably plenty of free antlers lying around the barn or garage.

Regardless of your tastes, brand affiliation or thoughts on various deer calls there is no arguing one point—they add another dimension to an activity we just can't get enough of. There's certainly nothing wrong with that.

Guide and call maker Joe Sears of Spencer, NY, says that antler rattling is effective much earlier in the season than most people suspect.

Chapter 15
Rattling is Effective If You Know When and Where

The wide 9-point rack rotated in the thick brush as its bearer searched for the source of the rattling noise that had drawn him. In a treestand 25 yards away Joe Sears relaxed his grip on the bowstring and reached over to gently tickle the tips together of his hanging rattling antlers.

The buck reacted immediately, stepping quickly to a small-opening 12 yards from Joe's stand. The late afternoon sun glinted off the wide rack as Joe drew and released the arrow. The buck bolted and disappeared into the thicket.

"He's down Joe!" yelled companion Jody Robertson moments later. Robertson was a client from Oklahoma for whom Sears had rattled in a 7-pointer earlier in the day and who was video taping Joe's hunt from a higher treestand.

Sears' lung-shot buck had piled up within 50 yards. The scene was in 1988 near the Ithaca Airport in Tompkins County, NY. The rack net-scored more than 130 inches and represented the first of two bucks that Joe Sears has put into the New York State Big Buck Club record book.

"That was the second day of the season, in the middle of October—way before the peak of the rut. That's the magic time for rattling," said Sears, who operates Adventure Game Calls and Guide Service in Spencer, NY. "Most guys think that the time to rattle is during the peak, the first or second week of November. But I think you'll find that to be too late. The bucks are usually all tied up with does then and are too busy to answer a challenge. They're not frustrated at that time and frustration is what makes rattling work."

Sears' log home and adjacent hunters lodge stand on a scenic Tioga County hilltop, surrounded by a virtual wildlife paradise.

Deer and turkey wander constantly within view of Sear's deck and afford him a year-round "laboratory" in which to observe wildlife actions and to test calls and theories.

"Almost any time in October is good for rattling, although conditions get better later in the month. October is when they're frustrated because they're through with their scraping but most of the does aren't ready and the boys are spoiling for a fight."

One October afternoon Sears rattled in four different bucks.

"Morning is always a good time but I've rattled in a lot of good bucks right in the middle of the day. They're active all day— on the prowl."

The quality of the herd and the number of mature, competitive bucks in the heavily-posted dairy country where Joe hunts probably makes rattling more effective than it might be on heavily-hunted (fewer bucks) areas. It also makes it a dandy spot for a guide and call maker to test techniques.

Unlike most rattling instructors and video makers, Joe does not use the grunt tube in conjunction with rattling.

"I'll quite often use sticks and rustle leaves to make it sound like a fight, but not the grunt," Sears said, despite the fact that Adventure Game Calls (PO Box 154, Spencer, NY 14833) sells grunt tubes. "I've never heard grunting during a buck fight and besides you've got enough to do going from rattling to getting your gun or bow without hassling with another implement.

"Don't get me wrong, the grunt tube has its place. I just don't think it's needed when rattling. I don't use the grunt tube unless I see a buck and want him to change direction. Unlike rattling, the grunt works real good during the peak of the rut. It doesn't always draw a buck to you but it may convince him that you're another deer."

Joe will some years spend an entire season using his adjustable grunt tube set only for a doe blat rather than the usual buck grunts. He's found bucks to be just as receptive to the sexual connotations of a doe vocalization as they were to the challenge represented by male grunts.

"It makes sense," said Sears, who started making calls and guiding hunters nearly 15 years ago and has made it his full-time occupation for the last six. "It's their breeding season. They're looking for a mate—that's their first objective. They'll react to a challenge out of frustration but the doe is much bigger attraction."

When setting up for rattling Sears says the wind is the biggest key. He likes to set up his stand downwind from a corner.

"Sometimes it's the corner of a thicket in a more open woods, other times it will be at the edge of a swamp or bedding area—some where on the edge of spot where a buck will feel comfortable moving because he's concealed."

While entire books and long magazine articles have examined the subject in great depth, Joe looks at rattling very simply. Take a set of antlers that's comfortable to carry and rattle, size and age being secondary considerations. Rattle them vigorously for two or three minutes. Stop for 30 seconds to a minute and do it again. Joe rattles more cautiously the second session because that's the way frustrated bucks go at it, employing more strategy than strength after evaluating their adversary in the first parry.

"It's easy to let your mind wander or to pay too much attention to rattling and technique when you should be alert for reaction," Joe said. "Sometimes a buck will run right in to the sound and other times he'll circle, checking the wind. But you've got to be alert.

"If you see him or hear a buck coming some guys want to give those horns one last tickle just to make sure—don't do it. If he's coming don't risk letting him see the movement. You should have the horns down and getting your bow. Remember, rattling is just a means to an end."

Many hunters feel that a deer munching vegetables placed as bait is a less desirable target than one feeding on natural browse.

Chapter 16
The Great Bait Debate

In most states the baiting of deer for hunting purposes is illegal and is viewed as unethical. But in those states where it is legal a debate rages over its effectiveness and ethics.

Michigan, with its 800,000 hunters, may be the hotspot of the debate. Hunting whitetails over bait piles is a widespread and controversial subject with the state's Department of Natural Resources merely an interested bystander.

"It's not a biological issue. It's not a safety issue. It's a social issue that the government has no business regulating," said a DNR spokesman from Lansing.

One side sees baiting as an unfair advantage—like snagging spawning salmon, a tactic that is legal in a few Great Lakes states but is fading fast. Others see baiting as providing better shot selection (fewer wounded animals); as providing an expedient means of hunting for those with little leisure time. They also see it as an aid in managing the deer population.

"To my way of thinking," said Dave Richey, longtime outdoors columnist at the Detroit News. "With baiting we've lost the hunting urge. It's been replaced by the urge to kill. Baiting offers very little hunting in the truest sense."

But it is big business. Unlike states like Wisconsin where bait piles are limited to a few square feet, Michigan's piles are unlimited. Richey surveyed a typical bait dealer ($60 per ton for sugar beets, $50 per ton for carrots) in 1993. The dealer filled 248 orders (ranging from one to five tons per order) on the day prior to the season.

The pro-baiting sportsmen argue that the improved positioning of the hunter over bait and the high harvest of does and immature deer (big bucks don't generally come to bait piles) are strong arguments for baiting. They point out that bait piles provide supplementary food sources for the animals.

Opponents of baiting say it fails to teach hunting. They say baiting turns deer nocturnal and changes patterns, makes poaching easier and generally cheapens the sport. They point out jurisdictional problems—people hunting pathways to and from bait piles that someone else has paid for and labored to put in place. They say deer become accustomed to human scent and are thus not as wary. They also point out the "garbage" problem represented by large piles of rotting vegetables and that the practice is fuel for anti-hunting sentiment.

"In some circles it's seen as an unfair advantage," Richey said. "Bait hunters need to question themselves about 'sporting chance'— could I be as successful if I hunted differently."

Surveys by the Michigan DNR have found that baiting is simply not that much more effective than other methods when you talk about hunting bucks. One survey showed that bait hunters took 3.7 bucks per 100 hunter days while 3.1 bucks were taken without baiting. In 1992 the state's success rate among firearms deer hunters was 52 percent over bait and 54 percent for other methods. Bowhunters enjoyed 51 percent success over bait and 54 percent using other methods.

"Driving is a much more effective method than baiting," said a DNR spokesman. "Hunting scrapes was shown to be more effective than baiting.

"Baiting wasn't much of an issue until the mid-1970s but it took off when we legalized treestands for archers (1975). Most gun hunters at the time didn't realize that baiting was legal for them."

DNR studies found no biological consequence to baiting. Deer are very selective eaters and bait piles didn't skew their nutritional intake as some anti-baiters predicted. Nor did the concentrations of deer caused by baiting lead to any disease problems. The studies also found that while a deer will wander slightly off its traditional migration path to go to a bait pile it will not stay long and won't wander more than a half-mile off the path before returning.

A Michigan survey of hunters in 1987 showed opinion on baiting divided evenly—one third supported baiting, one third was against and the other third had no opinion. In 1991 the same survey questions showed 41 percent approved of baiting, 24 percent disapproved and 35 percent didn't care.

Greg Gutschow, a spokesman for the 600,000-member Minnesota-based North American Hunting Club, noted that the club supports all legal means of hunting, recognizing the necessity that wildlife must be managed by different means in different areas.

But Gutschow also noted that baiting with vegetables is not the same as using scents or rattling to deer to attract them. Baiting is not natural, he contends, while the other means are.

"And we can't say that baiting is the same as hunting over agricultural fields or food plots," Gutschow said. "They are much larger and the hunter can never be sure were the deer is going to come out while a concentrated bait pile can be covered from all angles very easily."

Gutschow said that the widespread practice of baiting bears didn't get the same reaction as baiting deer because bear baiting "is necessary to significantly reduce the odds of encountering the animal. That's not so with deer."

He cited a 1979 Texas bowhunter study that showed hunting deer over bait piles showed only a 6 percent higher success rate than non-baiting methods but that the crippling losses were nearly double over bait.

And the Great Bait Debate rages on.

"The hunter perceives his prey with a singular affection and respect, maybe even a degree of reverence. And he alone is confronted with the paradox of inflicting violence and pain in a world he adores."

Chapter 17
Deer Search—Retrievers for Deer

The leaves are dry, the trail is cold and there are no stars or moonlight on this cloudy night. But the perky wirehaired dachshund's steady pull on the leash shows that she is maintaining her enthusiasm for the hunt better than her handler.

The trail started in a grown-over hayfield bordering an orchard, its debut pointed out just before dusk by the dismayed bowhunter who enlisted the handler's help. Digested food and bloodstains on the recovered arrow defined a paunch hit. The hunter had done what tracking he could, but that was nearly 14 hours ago.

The cold trail has taken them from the field, through a stand of hardwoods, a Christmas tree plantation, another woodlot, around a wet bottom, through the corner of meadow and now uphill into yet another stand of maples.

They are nearly three-quarters of a mile from the field where they picked up the deer's blood trail, but the visible spoor died out more than a half-mile ago. They've had to rely solely on Assy's studied nose and instincts ever since.

The 8-year-old dachshund is obviously tiring, her short legs working in almost constant fashion for the past three hours. But the faint, familiar scent wafting through her damp nostrils—the odor that had all but died out three times earlier in the session before she found it again—fuels an inbred determination as she makes her way through the light understory and over rotting deadfalls.

A small blood smear on fallen sapling goes unnoticed in the beam cast by the handler's coonhunter helmet light. But the sudden intensity of the scent the smear engenders flares in Assy's nostrils and she darts ahead, obviously excited. Her enthusiasm is restrained only by the handler's 30-foot leash.

Suddenly she stops and barks twice, her location hidden by darkness. The hunter moves forward until the light beam falls on

the object of their quest—the still form of the 6-point buck the hunter had arrowed that morning.

"You can't imagine the feeling of excitement and satisfaction when that leash goes limp and you look up and see the deer you've been tracking," says Deer Search Inc. handler Hans Klein of Salt Point, NY.

"It's actually an extension of the excitement of hunting."

The hunter perceives his prey with a singular affection and respect, maybe even a degree of reverence. And he alone is confronted with the paradox of inflicting violence and pain in a world he adores.

For these reasons, failing to recover a wounded deer is one of the most sickening experiences a hunter can endure.

The experience dredges up a gamut of negative emotions—frustration, anger, humiliation, pity and doubt of one's abilities. And never is this paradox more vivid than when a hunter has inflicted pain and violence in vain.

But it does happen—more often than we care to admit—and we owe it to the animal and to the sport to be as efficient as possible in its pursuit.

HUMAN TRACKERS NEED HELP

As trackers, however, humans outside the Third World are very limited. We've evolved away from such skills and definitely need help.

In most states outside the southeast the elements of dogs and deer hunting aren't a legal mix. But applying the canine element after the fact is demonstrably effective, where allowed.

In 1990 New York allowed statewide licensing of dog handlers for the specific task of tracking wounded or injured big game animals.

For the previous 15 years certified trackers were allowed to operate with special scientific collection permits. But the controls were so tight and application so specific that the practice was virtually limited to Dutchess and Suffolk Counties where Deer Search Inc. plied its craft.

Deer Search Inc. is a tightly knit non-profit group of experienced and dedicated dog handlers who have been exercising the largely European craft of big game trailing with dogs since 1975.

Hofstra University professor John Jeanneney is the grandfather of Deer Search. He first heard of the concept, as it's used in Germany, from Alsacan forestry students and decided to start a research project and pilot program in the mid-1960s.

Jeanneney, Poughkeepsie IBM engineer Klein and Don Hickman, an operating engineer from Pleasant Valley, founded Deer Search in 1975 and incorporated in 1977.

Today the group has almost 60 members and has recovered more than 1,000 deer and a few bear—over the last 19 hunting seasons.

The recovery rate hovers at around 30 percent—less than one-fourth of the bowshot deer tracked and one-third of the gun-wounded animals.

At first glance the recovery figures may not be impressive. But consider that the track is seldom less than 12 hours old, usually has been diluted or compromised by age and/or weather, wind, dew and previous tracking attempts, and is engaged only after a human tracker has exhausted all hope in finding the animal itself.

Many sorties are terminated when it turns out that the pursued animal is not mortally wounded, or when it is discovered that an animal has moved to property to which the trackers cannot gain access. Particularly in the cases of deer with sealed arrow wounds, the dog sometimes shifts to another deer without the handler realizing it.

"We encourage hunters to track their own deer and often give them advice over the phone," Jeanneney noted in a report. "We go in with our dogs only when all else fails."

NO EASY RECOVERIES

There are simply no easy recoveries for Deer Search. Blame it on our hunting heritage.

"In Germany a hunter considers it proper procedure to call immediately for a guide and tracking dog if a deer just shot does not fall within 100 meters," Jeanneney noted.

"In contrast, the camouflaged American bowhunter . . . could not respect himself as a hunter if he did not do everything in his power to find the deer on his own."

Until the mid-1980s virtually all of Deer Search's membership resided in Dutchess and Suffolk Counties. But publicity and the eventual agreement by the Department of Environmental Conservation to license the concept statewide has added members from Long Island, the northern Catskills and from as far west in the state as Hamburg and Rochester. There are even members from Wisconsin.

"The (Deer Search) members are very dedicated and sincere in what they do," said John Proud, NYDEC Region 7 Wildlife Manager and a member of the committee that helped organize statewide licensing for deer-tracking dog handlers.

"I think their dedication and integrity in how they went about things did a lot to sell what for us was a totally foreign concept. Their input was essential to us."

Glenn Cole, NYDEC Region 3 Wildlife Manager, has been at his current office since 1968 and has been familiar with Deer Search since Jeanneney applied for his first collection permit in the 1960s.

Due to Cole's proximity and familiarity with Deer Search (he's had two deer recovered by the group in three tries), he was considered the leading authority on the concept among wildlife managers.

"I had a different perspective than the other members of the committee," Cole said. "I knew what these guys (Deer Search) stood for and how they conducted things."

Once the law was voted in to permit licensing, the NYDEC had to draft regulations.

"The regulations had to be drafted totally within the department in an area where we (biologists and experts) had no experience," Proud said from his Cortland office.

"Just the opposite, in fact. The Conservation Code specifically prohibits using dogs for big game. And there was no other state in North America that we could draw information from."

The state gave its first licensing examination for potential deer-tracking dog handlers in 1990. The examination is made up of questions determined by Deer Search and members of various state agencies. It tests the applicants' knowledge of Fish and Wildlife law and regulations that govern the use of licensed leashed tracking dogs.

Also included are questions on the taking and possession of big game animals, dog care, weapons safety , training and handling methods and areas of knowledge appropriate for leashed dog handlers.

The annual exam is now held in August. There is a $25 non-refundable application fee for the exam and the license, good for five years, costs $100 and can be renewed for $125.

In New York, the licensed tracker must also hold a valid state hunting license and may only use a dog certified and licensed as required by the Agriculture and Markets Law.

"In my view it's going to take a while for this concept to catch on," Proud says. "Training and using a dog to trail wounded deer is very labor intensive.

"The guys in Deer Search are very dedicated. It would definitely test the meddle of most dog handlers I know."

State-licensed trackers may charge a fee for their services if they also hold a New York State guide's license. Members of Deer Search Inc. do not charge for their services, but do accept donations.

"We didn't want to go that route (charging a fee) because we felt that if someone couldn't afford the fee they wouldn't call us," Klein said.

"We use the donations to buy liability insurance coverage from the NRA and to pay mileage to our trackers. I've gone on calls and got nothing after finding a deer for a guy who couldn't afford it. And I've gotten $60 or $70 from other guys for a couple of hours when the deer wasn't even found. It sort of evens out."

Past experience in tracking big game with dogs was taken into consideration in the state licensing program.

"There were 30 or 40 people operating under special collecting permit 1105–15 who were working on our licensing program," said Chris von Schilgen, principal wildlife technician and assistant to NYDEC special licensing unit leader Pat Martin.

"Those people were grandfathered in upon written request."

BACKGROUND SEARCH REQUIRED

Deer Search requirements are substantially more rigid than the state's licensing criteria. The group charges only a $10 initiation fee and $5 annual dues but applicants must sign an agreement that allows a search of his or her criminal background.

Certified trackers, you see, are allowed to work at night, using lights. Those with handgun permits are also allowed to use them—provided they are at least .35 caliber with at least a four-inch barrel—to dispatch wounded animals.

The state is understandably reluctant to bestow such privileges on anyone who might have even the slightest inclination toward illegal acts.

"If a guy is trailing a wounded spike and a 10-pointer jumps out of its bed in front of him, we've got to know he's not going to shoot it," Cole says.

To become certified as a handler by Deer Search, applicants must go on six calls during which he or she handles the dog, interviews the hunter, contacts state police and game wardens and tracks and locates the deer—all under the watchful eyes of a Master Tracker.

Deer Search Inc.-certified dogs are tested on a W-shaped course that consists of a one-pint blood trail laid out over a 1,000-yard course and aged at least 20 hours.

Although the state does not specify any particular breed of dog for big-game tracking, Deer Search members prefer wirehaired dachshunds.

In addition to a keen nose and huge heart, the size (13–20

pounds) of these dogs facilitates carrying them back to the last sign.

"It was also easier to sell the conservation department on using small dogs that couldn't run down a wounded deer if it came upon one," Klein says.

Selling the state on the use of dogs to track deer hasn't been a cakewalk, at any rate. The Agriculture and Markets division, which licenses dogs, had some concerns, as did the State Police and NYDEC.

Deer Search found former DEC Wildlife Bureau Chief Stuart Free to be receptive and helpful in their lobbying efforts. But when Free retired three years ago, the attitude changed.

"For a while the new administration maintained the idea that using dogs to track wounded deer wasn't part of the hunting ethic," Klein says.

But the lobbying eventually worked, legislation was passed in 1989 and the NYDEC set up statewide licensing guidelines in 1991.

Deer Search today annually recovers more than 100 wounded deer. In 1975 they recovered five.

The group, which has spread the word about its services for years from booths at outdoor shows, has implemented a dispatch system.

"The telephone number that we advertise in our flier can be transferred to anyone's home phone," Klein says. "Each member takes a certain number of days as dispatcher and knows exactly how many handlers are available at any time."

Thanks to the dedication and perservance of a handful of Hudson Valley dog handlers, the trail of a wounded deer no longer ends with the visible sign.

FOR INFORMATION ON DEER SEARCH:

For information on Deer Search, Inc., write Secretary Patricia Chapman, RR 1 Box 379, Stamfordville, NY 12581 or call Hans Klein at 914–635–3961.

The group accepts inquiries from anyone interested, regardless of their state of residence. There are quiet lobbying efforts in several states to institute systems patterned after Deer Search.

Of course the organization's history, success and strict training give it credibility beyond New York's borders but will also be difficult to duplicate when other states endeavor to build their own deer-tracking systems.

TRACKING WITH THE MASTERS

The use of dogs to track wounded big game has its roots in Europe. As a German born in Austria, Klein was well acquainted with the craft's European heritage.

Thus, when the opportunity presented itself in October, 1989, the Deer Search veteran entered his 7-year-old wirehaired dachshund, Assy, in the 32nd Verbandschweisspruefung am Hoherodskopf one of the toughest bloodtracking tests in Germany.

Assy, imported from Germany as a 3-month puppy, was an American field champion and two-time Prize One winner in Deer Search competitions. She was in her prime, Klein reasoned. And successful participation in the German test would the first step in qualifying him as an international Jagdgebrauchshundverband judge for blood-tracking trials.

Klein and Assy flew from New York to Frankfurt and drove to the village of a friend, who had prepared a 20-hour-old 1,200-meter test line for Assy to acclimate where with the conditions and presence of strange scents such as roe deer, boar and red stag.

She performed well and two days later the duo found themselves in competition in Hochwaldhausen, site of the heralded test. Assy found the planted roe buck in 90 minutes, passed the 20-hour blood test with a Prize Two award and was the only dog of the seven entered to pass.

The traditional fir bow was awarded by the judges, which Klein split between his hat and Assy's collar.

Klein now hopes to stage Jagdgebrauchshundverband tests in New York in order to better spread the knowledge and spirit of his craft internationally.

Chapter 18
Star Gazing for Wildlife

Human knowledge of the universe is so minute that the skies remain the ultimate mystery.

Strange happenings, from mass murders to mass births, from temporary insanity to flashes of inspirational brilliance, are laid to celestial influence. A large section of society lets horoscopes pattern their lives.

The forces that govern the ocean and tides are inarguably linked to gravitational changes caused by the alignment of the sun and the moon. Since nearly two-thirds of the earth is covered by water, one might assume that all life on the planet is affected by these tidal forces.

"There hasn't been any scientific study on it that I'm aware of," said wildlife biologist Mike Hall. "But I don't doubt that there is some effect. It certainly does effect humans; just drop by a hospital emergency room on the night of a full moon."

"If you could find the answer and bottle it, you'd be rich."

Well, some people do "bottle" the idea and sell it in the form of fish and game activity tables in newpapers and magazines.

There are hunters who swear by them and others that swear at them. Some wouldn't leave home without the predicted "major feeding times" while others see them as another voodoo gimmick designed to prey on the bankrolls of the gullible.

Several newspaper outdoor writers, while pooh-poohing the veracity of the syndicated prediction tables, noted the public outcry whenever the newspaper neglected to print that week's edition.

Like fish scents, horse racing betting formulas, horoscopes and fishing's Color C-Lector, there are times when the tables seem to work. Anyone who pays attention to such a tool wants them to work, and that feeling of hope is no small part of what makes the outdoors quest so enjoyable.

There is little doubt that lunar movements key whitetail movements—but how predictable are they?

Various tables are syndicated throughout the country, the most famous probably being the Solunar Tables, which have run in Field & Stream magazine since 1937. They were developed by Pennsylvanian John Alden Knight, supposedly on information gleaned from an Indian bass fishing guide in Georgia during the formative years of this century.

Jacqueline Knight, the widow of John Knight's son, still "locks herself away and figures the tables with a pad and pencil," according to a Solunar spokesman.

Another company claims that a former Chesapeake market hunter came up with its formula. An Outdoor Life article a few years ago credited yet another table to the Maori Indians of New Zealand. The Solunar spokesman noted that the calculations are based on data gleaned from the Greenwich Observatory in England, from U.S. governmental data and that of several naval bases.

"There really aren't any trade secrets," said John Aldridge of Vektor, a computerized fish and game activity table distributed by the North American Hunting Club of Minnesota.

"The data that our computer calculations are based on is available from the U.S. Government Title Office in Bethesda, Maryland. It's publication no. 97, the Table of Harmonic Tides."

Aldridge said that calculators pick a specific geographic spot—he uses a point just east of St. Louis and, he said, Solunar uses a spot in New York Harbor—to use as a reference point and handicaps all the data to conform to points east and west of that.

The formula, Aldridge said, takes into consideration 36 constituent forces, the majors being, "the sun, moon and a couple of planets.

"Although it's very complicated, basically the major times listed are when the moon is directly on the other side of the world from that spot. The minor times are when the moon is at right or left angles to that spot.

"Probably the most troubling aspect is that most of the tables contradict each other; the predicted major and minor activity times being radically different.

"All offer disclaimers that local influences, such as weather and habitat conditions, can override the urges supposedly caused by these dark forces.

"How can they all be different when we're all using the same information? That's a good question," Aldridge said.

"I'd like to get everybody involved to put up their calculations for a hunting and fishing contest to see who is the most accurate.

"But of course that might prove inconclusive, too . . ."

The ethics of sportsmanship is not a fixed code, but must be formulated and practiced by the individual, with no referee but the Almighty.   —Aldo Leopold

PART V:

THE HUNTERS' TOOLS

Chapter 19
Let's Sight Your Gun In

We had a deal. Dad promised to teach me the art of shooting if I survived the first 10 years of life.

Fair enough. Of course there were certain other stipulations—mostly vows of good conduct, closer attention to personal hygiene, school work and chores, lessened hostilities toward siblings, etc.—but to me age was the biggie.

My 10th birthday arrived about two days short of eternity and, after the obligatory birthday cake and feigned gratitude over new socks and underwear, I dutifully reminded Dad of our agreement. That sunny spring afternoon we packed his 16-gauge Savage and a fistful of rifled slugs into the old station wagon and headed down our dirt road to the neighbor's farm.

Years of helplessly watching the family hunters come and go; of pressing my nose against windows of gun stores; of staring into gun cabinets and magazines, melted away in the half-mile trip to Max's back pasture.

After rudimentary instruction on the safe handling of a firearm—which I more or less ignored in the excitement of the impending moment—we reached what shall be romantically referred to as the moment of truth.

It was time to touch one off.

The target was a coffee can perched on a fence post about 20 yards away. I wrestled the 9-pound gun to a rest on a stump, sighted down the barrel and gave the trigger a quick, excited yank.

My next remembrance was being sprawled on the ground, dazed, bicep bruised and throbbing. To find my nose, one could follow a distinct blood trail across my youthful visage to a heretofore vacant area somewhere above my right eyebrow.

"You missed."

Dad's voice was barely perceptible over the loud ringing in my ears.

Sighting in a rifle or shotgun from a bench is relatively simple when conducted at short ranges.

Before shooting for accuracy, make sure all scope and action screws are torqued down tightly.

"If you're going to try it again, hold it tighter against your shoulder and lean into it—like I said the first time," he said, apparently oblivious to my condition.

Dad was into the old "sink or swim" theory. Today they call it aptitude testing. He would lead you to a certain point, but always let you experience the situation first hand. You were the judge.

If you wanted to try again after that, he was there to instruct and guide. If not, he didn't force the issue. When I reached for the gun again, he knew that had my undivided attention, and launched into a full-blown course on safety and proper shooting techniques. I was, needless to say, a model student and have refined my shooting technique somewhat in the subsequent years.

Here's some tips for you:

SIGHT-IN UP CLOSE TO START

You're well aware that you may encounter 250- or 300-yards shots in the area where you're going to be hunting but the only range available to sight your rifle is limited to 50 yards. How can you sight in?

First, make sure the bore is absolutely clean. That's the foundation on which to build accuracy. Next, make sure that every screw on your mounts, rings—even the trigger guard—is as tight as possible. Remember that over-tightening some action screws can be detrimental. Make sure you have a steady rest. I use a portable Benchmark shooting rig that features a cushioned rest, adjustable legs and arm and a strap across the gun butt that helps absorb and distribute recoil.

Draw the stock tightly back to your shoulder and pull the forearm of the gun backward and down firmly. Both the forearm and stock should be resting on energy-absorbing material.

When foundation has been laid, set up your target at 25 yards for a scoped rifle or 12.5 yards for a centerfire rifle with iron sights. The short range makes spotting and adjustments easy—and at the same time you are approximating where the bullet will strike the same target if it were 200 to 300 yards down range.

Because your sights or scope are mounted on the top of the barrel, above the line of sight, your gun is positioned to shoot slightly upward to compensate. The bullet leaves the bore in such a manner that is actually rises above the sight line, travels in an arc and drops back below it as gravity works on it down range.

Ballistics charts show, for example, that a scope-sighted .270 firing 130-grain factory loads at about 3,100 feet per second, zeroed at 25 yards, will group three inches high at 100 yards, four inches high at 200 and dead-on at 275. A similarly scoped .30-06 shooting 150-grain factory loads at .2,700 fps zeroed at 25 yards will be almost three inches high at 100, a bit over two inches at 200 and back to the point of aim at 250 yards.

The gun should be fine-tuned at 100 yards, but the shorter range sighting will get you close if that's all that's available. One caution: When you sight a rifle, the resultant accuracy pattern is good only for that exact configuration of scope or sight, load and bullet type. Any change in sight height, load or bullet type will grossly exaggerate differences down range.

BOOST POWER TO SHRINK GROUPS

Used properly, a variable-power scope on your rifle or shotrgun can not only tell you a lot about your firearm but also about yourself as a shooter.

Sure, cranking up the power comes in handy when you want to check out the rack on that buck that just stepped out on the other side of the bean field. But it also has other uses.

Increasing the power of your scope will also help shrink your groups at the range

With the increased resolution you will be able to tell if you're holding in exactly the same place every shot. Increased resolution will also show quickly if the crosshairs are moving where at a lower power you might have thought you were holding rock-steady.

The increased resolution might not be as important with a rifle that shoots into two inches at 100 yards as it would be with a tack-driver. If you miss your hold by a quarter-inch with a two-inch rifle, you've only increased your group by 25 percent. But miss by a quarter inch with a rifle capable of half-inch groups and you've doubled the groups.

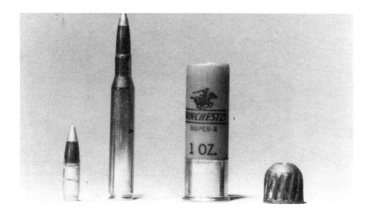

Chapter 20
The Argument Over Bullet Performance

"The hunting arrow kills by hemorrhage. You want it to slice cleanly through the body," said the lecturer. "But a bullet kills by shock. You want a bullet that stays in the deer and transfers all of its energy."

Not really, sir. Both actually kill by tissue destruction. The arrow is designed to promote hemorrhage, yes—via tissue destruction. Passing through the body is preferred in that case because it promotes a better blood trail.

A bullet does not kill with shock, however. It too kills by tissue destruction.

The fact that anyone would judge a bullet's lethality by whether or not it stayed in the body is folly. But I'm a little soft on the argument. A friend of mine, respected gun writer Bryce Towsley, is a little more vitriolic.

"I find it irresponsible," growls the passionate bearded New Englander.

Bryce uses the example of the .22 long rifle cartridge to show

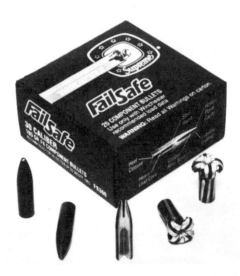

Winchester's Fail Safe bullet is a prime example of today's controlled expansion bullets that retain their weight but cause prodigious tissue damage and hydrastatic shock.

how ridiculous the "stay in the body" claim really is.

A .22 long rifle will indeed dump all of its energy in the deer, and the spent projectile will remain in the body.

"Does that make it a deer caliber?" Bryce asks. "Of course not."

Bryce acknowledges that if a centerfire caliber offers the same performance they can be very effective. But there are simply too many variables such as impact velocity, bullet path, game size, material penetrated, and the physiological variables of the target animals for such a general statement to be always true.

Follow Bryce's logic. My .22-250 with a 55-grain boattail bullet will cut the air at about 3,900 fps and deliver nearly 1,400 foot pounds of energy at 100 yards. I know people who use it as a deer caliber and indeed the energy at 100 yards is well above the industry-accepted lethality minimum of 1,200 for deer-sized game. Drill a whitetail in the lungs or center one in the neck and you'll make venison. Catch the shoulder and you've probably made a cripple that you might not find.

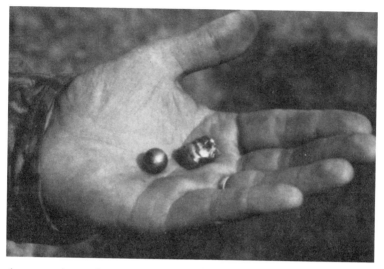

A comparison of an unfired and recovered blackpowder round ball shows the effectiveness of the load. A round ball needs a velocity of at least 1,250 feet per second in order to expand on impact.

As Bryce points out, the bullet dumped its energy in the deer's body and stayed there. A high-speed varmint round, like the aforementioned .22-250, .220 Swift, etc. is designed for flat trajectory over extended range and for immediate expansion upon impact. They simply disintegrate—a full expenditure of energy, to be sure—but it's designed to be lethal on tiny framed varmints, not 150-pound ungulates. They are designed to please pelt hunters who want the bullet to explode inside and not leave a ragged exit hole to sew up.

Bryce acknowledges that most popular centerfire cartridges are over-kill for whitetails and even the poorest can thus dispatch a deer. But the low-end choices put a lot more emphasis on luck and fate than ballistics and sooner or later one of those variables mentioned earlier will jump up and bite you.

So you want pass-through, right? Not necessarily. A bullet that blows through an animal without expanding is similarly ineffective. Remember, you want tissue damage. That means expansion of the bullet in the body. The bullet needs to expand early and retain its weight as it tears through tissue and exit via a large, ragged hole under all but the most extreme conditions.

The expansion ensures that the "wide body" will transfer energy to the surrounding tissue—called hydrostatic shock. The weight retention and bullet integrity enhance penetration and its ability to retain its original course after impact.

Bullet construction is thus an essential element in a good deer load. Its weight, ballistic coefficient and makeup are all considerations. Its weight must be sufficient that it retains energy not only in the air but also after impact (remember the 55-grain .22-250's speed but relative inadequacy upon impact?). At longer distances, (200 yards and more) pointed bullets are better because they have a higher ballistic coefficient. In practical terms ballistic coefficient is an index of the bullet's ability to cut through the air. In mathematical terms it's something like a ratio of the bullet's weight to the product of the bullet's diameter squared and form factor.

Got that? Me either. I let the chronograph or manufacturer's chart tell me the BC and make a decision on a comparative basis.

"The higher the BC the better the velocity retention and wind-bucking ability of the bullet," says shooting expert Joe Ventimiglia, president of Venco Industries, makers of Shooter's Choice gun care products. "A short, stubby bullet that sheds velocity quickly has a low BC while a long, slender bullet built for long-range shooting will have a high BC.

For example a .30-caliber, 180-grain Sierra flat-base bullet has a BC of .501 while a slightly less pointed 180-grain Speer flat-base is .435. Performance is quite similar, although the Sierra has a slight edge in velocity retention.

By way of contrast a .30-caliber, 180-grain round-nosed Speer bullet has a BC of only .288. The trajectory is far more looping, but that's unimportant because such a bullet is designed for relatively close-range shooting where its shape and mass help it retain its integrity upon impact.

But again, BC isn't much of a factor for shooting inside of 200 yards. The thickness, hardness and taper of a bullet's jacket affect the rate and degree of expansion. So do the hardness of the core nd its exposure at the nose. Mid-weight soft-nosed bullets in the .257 to .358 range are suitable for deer hunting with most cartridges. You'll want heavy .243 or 6mm bullets but relatively lightweight softpoints for the big-bore cases. It's important to match bullets to cases. For example, bullets made to open at .30-30 velocities come unglued if you use them up close in a Mondo .300-magnum load.

Controlled expansion bullets are high-tech, masterfully designed, very expensive and totally unneeded for deer hunting. Yes, I recommend Nosler partitions to elk hunters I guide in Idaho, but that's because their construction allows the bases to blow through heavy elk bone and sinew. Traditional, low-price soft points are plenty for deer-sized game. In fact they may be slightly more accurate and yield superior results on deer. If its got the right energy, expands and retains its weight the bullet is doing its job and there is no need for the high-tech controlled expansion unit for a relatively lightweight target like a deer.

In fact, in extremely long shooting (over 400 yards), the cheaper off-the-shelf bullets often out-perform the expensive ones. Controlled expansion bullets, you see, need a certain minimum velocity in order to leaf-out as designed. If the bullet slows to below that speed the expensive brand will poke a hole rather than blast one but the softer, simpler inexpensive loads will expand regardless.

TEMPERATURE, ALTITUDE ARE VARIABLES

Consider, also that other variables will effect the velocity of your load, which in turn effect energy and trajectory.

If you're hunting in freezing temperatures, for example, don't expect your loads to group at the same spot they did when you sighted them during the summer.

I guided my brother-in-law, Dean Sunderland of Phoenix, Arizona, on a December whitetail hunt in northern Idaho in the early 1990s. Dean and I have more in common than marrying a set of sisters. He's an inveterate hunter and an absolute firearms freak. If it goes boom, Dean's probably got a couple and shoots them often.

Well at Shattuck Creek Ranch and Outfitters we request that all of our hunters take advantage of the town range in Elk River, Idaho, to check the zero on their guns.

Dean was shooting a Winchester Model 70 in .270 with handloads that he'd made up to print 2.5 inches high at 100 yards. That was 2.5 inches high at 100 yards in Phoenix. You know, 100 degrees and dry. Well, in 30-degree temperatures at 3,000 feet above sea level the load was consistently hitting below zero—more than three inches low—at 100 yards.

The difference? Chamber pressure. The cold effects the metal, making tolerances change and chamber pressure drops. When pressure drops, so does velocity and when velocity drops . . . well, you know the drill.

On the other hand, chamber pressure can also be boosted. As a bullet enters the rifling and seals off the bore, the chamber pressure is at or approaching maximum. Just where peak pressure occurs is most often dependent upon the type of powder used. Other factors, however, may enter the picture.

A badly fouled or leaded barrel will boost chamber pressure, leading to erratic or even dangerous situations.

ALL BARRELS AREN'T THE SAME

It's imperative to test any bullet in your own rifle. Rifles of the same design, even make and caliber can perform entirely differently with the same load. The twist rate of the rifling, for instance, is a variable that must be considered. As a general rule of thumb a slower, longer-length bullet needs a faster twist than its quick but short counterpart.

You should note, also, that factory-issued ballistics will most often be superior to what you achieve with your own gun. Thus a factory ballistics table's energy and trajectory charts won't be accurate for your gun.

Yes the factory ballistics are accurate, but not under the conditions that you and I shoot. The factory runs its tests in climate-controlled, windless tunnels using 26- or 28-inch pressure barrels that are longer and tighter than sporting barrels. That means higher pressure, which in turn means higher velocity—which effects energy and trajectory.

Barrels less than 26 inches often don't allow full potential because all the powder isn't burned before the bullet leaves the muzzle.

A 20-inch barrel, for example, will give about 95 percent of the velocity of a 26-inch barrel with identical loads. Losses can range from 20 to 40 fps per inch of barrel length for medium-velocity cartridges and 50 to 60 fps per inch for larger magnums.

Chapter 21
Let's Keep it Clean, Gang

Cleaning a gun after a day of shooting is like washing dishes after a great meal. It's a necessary chore that's viewed as drudgery—sort of payment for the enjoyment previously received.

While everyone knows that their guns should be cleaned regularly, it is probably the most neglected aspect of shooting. Afterall, we also know the value of flossing, low fat diets, regular exercise and safe sex.

Heavy fouling has undoubtedly retired more guns than worn barrels. Nothing destroys a gun's groups or pattern faster or ruins a barrel sooner than fouling.

Fresh fouling may look fairly innocent when viewed in the bore. But you should realize that powder and primer residue gets burnt and ironed into the walls of the bore everytime a bullet passes over it. Copper and lead are left in the barrel in the form of a thin, smeared wash.

It can start to get serious in high-velocity guns after only 15-20 shots. That might represent years for the average weekend hunter but can be only a matter of minutes on a bench or overlooking a varmint field.

Fouling starts with the first shot and increases every time you squeeze the trigger. The result in rifles is a sandwich effect of powder and gilded metals and in shotguns it's powder and melted plastic. The fouling attracts moisture and traps it against the barrel walls. What follows with time obviously isn't good.

In a rifle, particularly one that handles loads faster than 3,000 fps, the effect is magnified. Each shot literally irons the residue into the rifling grooves. In extreme cases it hardens it into a compound that can be harder than the barrel steel.

At that point, removing the heinous mixture from your barrel can

A rifle or shotgun should be cleaned from the breech end whenever possible and the barrel should always be tilted downward to keep solvent from running into the action and wood.

A coated, single-piece rod like this one from Dewey Manufacturing is best. Aluminum rods tend to pick up grit that can actually score the barrel. A bore guide like this one is also a good idea.

be next to impossible without damaging the rifling. As it builds it actually sizes the bullets and accuracy goes south in the proverbial handbasket.

Shotgunners see their patterns similarly go awry for much the same reason. Powder and plastic wad fouling reach a point where they drag on subsequent shotcups and pull them away from loads, thus negating their controlling, containing function.

Now outdoor writers are supposedly experts in all matters pertaining to firearms, shooting, hunting, fishing, etc. In actuality, however, no one can be an expert in all things. A good outdoor writer simply knows where to get expert information.

In my case, when looking for shooting information, I go to folks obssessed with firearms performance—benchrest shooters.

These guys are the test pilots of the shooting industry. Their research, testing, tinkering and application has contributed much to the general sport of rifle shooting.

One of the main contributions is the notion that a sanitary bore and proper techniques to achieve it are absolute necessities.

In a pursuit where a five-shot 100-yard group that can't be covered with a dime sends the competitor into apoplexy, precision is a hallmark. It only follows that absolutely clean barrels are a prerequisite.

The same reasoning pertains to all firearms of course—accumulated carbon, copper, lead and plastic shotgun wad fouling changes tolerances and effects accuracy. Like a race car, no gun can achieve its true potential without clear track to run on.

EVOLUTION OF BORE CLEANER

When Nitrobenzene was eliminated from bore cleaners (a move we should all applaud for health and environmental reasons), benchrest shooters began to experiment.

"Guys tried everything from home brews to blackpowder solvent, spray engine cleaner—even jewelers abrasive," said veteran bench rest competitor Sal Ventimiglia of Chagrin Falls, Ohio.

Some early solvents were so strong they would pit or gall stainless steel barrels. Others took hours to work.

Ventimiglia's personal "home brew" solvent was so effective and efficient that it gained widespread acceptance among fellow shooters. So widespread, in fact, that it was the basis for the Shooter's

Choice line of gun care products, marketed today by Sal's sons, Joe and Frank.

Shooter's Choice is just one of many effective product lines designed for today's shooters. In addition to conventional bore solvents there are also specialty blends today, such as copper removers for shooters of high-speed jacketed loads. Sweets 7.62, Hoppes BenchRest and Shooter's Choice Copper Remover probably head the field there.

GUN CLEANING TIPS:

In talking with Ventimiglia and other benchrest types I was able to glean the following pointers:

The first consideration is a good cleaning rod and the appropriate jag. The rod is the last place that you want to cut corners to save a few cents. Get a good one. Vinyl-coated rods like Deweys are by far the best and some blackpowder shooters prefer nylon. Both afford protection for the crown, leade and rifling.

Stay away from hardened steel jointed rods. Jointed aluminum rods are similarly unhealthy. A soft metal like aluminum can pick up grit and act just like a lap, scratching the lands and grooves of a rifled barrel with every stroke.

For shotguns, smoothbores or rifled barrels, an excellent patch rod can be made from a 5/8ths-inch wooden dowel with a bicycle handlebar grip fastened to one end. An absorbent paper towel (we've found Bounty brand works best) folded and rolled to bore-filling diameter is an excellent shotgun cleaning patch.

Soak the towel with a quality bore cleaner and push it the length of the bore from chamber to muzzle. Wet brush and wet patch until clean.

Use only phosphorus bronze brushes wound on a core for shotguns or rifles. Stainless steel brushes are so hard they will score some barrel steel.

If you're serious about accuracy and barrel life, use a bore guide. Not only does a guide fitted into the bolt slot assure that the rod and brush/jag are concentric to the bore at all times (providing best protection and most efficient strokes) but it also keeps solvent from dripping into the trigger mechanicism or bedding.

Always use a rest to hold the firearm steady while the cleaning rod is worked. The rest should have padding to protect the finish and should be built so that the muzzle is lower than the receiver so that solvents drain away from the chamber and stock wood.

You can go with anything from a top-end Sinclair jig or an inexpensive MTM Caseguard. The muzzle-down angle and sturdy hold is the key.

Of course it's aways advisable to clean from the chamber to the muzzle and never try to reverse the stroke before the brush passes completely out of the barrel.

The rule of thumb among riflemen is to make one pass with the solvent-soaked brush for every shot that was fired since the last cleaning. Handloaders will find that different powders leave different amounts of residue, depending on their burning rate.

If they're headed home, bench rest shooters will often run a dry patch to catch loose fouling, then a wet patch and leave the bore in that state for storage. Residue is lifted and suspended in the solvent, which also displaces moisture until the next time you shoot. A dry patch, at least, will be needed before the next time the rifle is shot.

Remember that the rods should always be wiped clean and the brushes should have solvent rinsed out of them. Solvent is meant, afterall, to dissolve gilded metal and doesn't know the difference between residue and a bronze or brass bristles.

Clean brushes with something like MEK or Shooter's Choice Quick Scrub spray.

In rifles or shotguns use a toothbrush to scrub bearing surfaces with bore solvent to clean actions and bearing surfaces. Then wipe it off, spray with a degreaser and coat the metal surfaces (including the inside of the tube) with a quality moisture displacent.

When using a grease or oil lubricant the rule of thumb is "if you can see it, it's too much." Use sparingly and always check the temperature range on the product label. If the range isn't listed, chances are you're holding something that turns into gunk in extreme cold weather.

THE TRUTH BEHIND TEFLON

The use and success of Polytetrafluoroethylene (PTFE), widely referred to as Teflon (TM) has been extraordinary and has provided technological advancement in many areas. But its use in gun care applications and as an automotive additive has caused controversy.

A bullet is like a race car—it needs a clean track in order to reach its full performance potential.

Chemists tell us that surface preparation is crucial to the effectiveness of PTFE—it must adhere to the surface it is to protect. The surface preparation includes an involved and critical process of vapor degreasing, grit blasting and a coating with a manganese phosphate.

This can be achieved and is very effective in coating cooking utensils and tools. But even then PTFE is not recommended if the treated surfaces will experience high loading or extreme pressure conditions—two major factors in firearms use and internal combustion engines.

"In a case where PTFE is added directly to an existing oil, there is no surface preparation, which is critical to the effectiveness of the polymer," said lubrication engineer-chemist George Fennell of Butler, Pa.

"When PTFE and other solid-film lubricants are used in their proper manners along with the proper surface preparation and application, they can be of enormous tribological benefit," Fennell said. "When misused or misapplied, they can either do nothing or become a real detriment to the system, probably resulting in the latter."

CONDITIONING A RIFLE BARREL

A rifleman can avoid a whole lot of future hassles, or right a bunch of previous wrongs with a simple exercise known as conditioning the barrel.

Take a new rifle, or an old one that hasn't been treated real well, to the range and clean it thoroughly.

Then shoot a round, clean it, shoot another, clean it, and so on until you've burned up 10-15 rounds. Continue but clean after every two rounds for the next 20-25.

In a new gun you're actually lapping the barrel with the bullet. In an older gun you may be loosening and cleaning out past indiscretions. In both cases you're conditioning the bore so that subsequent cleaning will be easier.

This exercise has made demonstrable improvements in the accuracy of previously mistreated guns, and even in guns right out of the box.

If you're concerned with accuracy or durability or future convenience, the bottom line is that a little tender loving care never hurt any relationship.

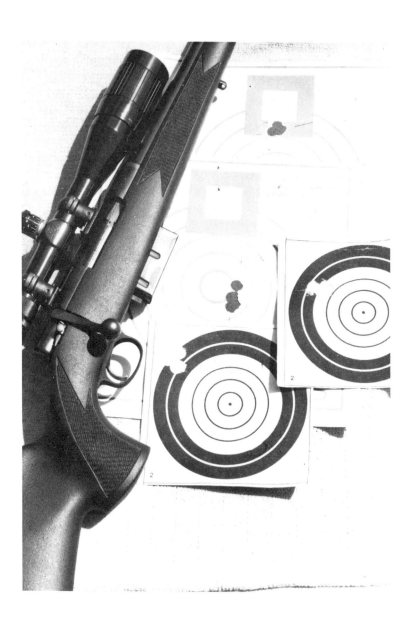

*Groups like this are everyone's goal, but most guns need some
work before tight groups are realized.*

Chapter 22:
What's Wrong With This Gun?

The breeze has died; the sight picture is steady, the rest solid.
Just exhale smoothly . . . steady pressure on the trigger. . . .

BANG!

It felt good. It looked good. All the criteria were met—should be
dead-on. Let's check the spotting scope.

Damn. One o'clock an inch outside the black. That makes for a
4-inch spread at 100 yards. It's a group, but only in technical terms.

You had in mind something under an inch—with nothing sticking
out. I mean four inches at 100 yards might be all right in a pinch, if
you're looking to catch a moose in the lungs at 50 feet. But you

Simple tightening of screws can often effect accuracy in a rifle.

had visions of dumping a buck in his tracks at 300 yards before he could step into the neighbor's posted pasture.

The only way this rifle would be a threat to deer would be if a bayonet were fitted.

Maybe you've heard that new barrels—particularly quality tubes—have to be "shot-in" to achieve their accuracy potential. Indeed, custom rifle makers will shoot a gun 150-200 times before delivery.

But simply "shooting-in" in an effort to shrink our 4-inch group to sub-MOA is like using Preparation H when surgery is in order.

No, it's going to take more than just shooting. Let's see, the gun cycles fine. It has a good scope with an adjustable objective (corrected parallax can mean up to a half-inch at 100 yards). You've tightened the screws on everything from the trigger guard to the scope rings.

You weren't letting it recoil on the sling studs where you? How about flinching? No, of course you wouldn't do that. So let's assume that gun and scope are set up right and we can eliminate human variables (a big assumption).

And let's also assume, to keep this chapter under novel length, that the load is at least in the right ball park. Dissertations on neck sizing, turning, tension; bullet seating, flash hole deburring, primers, powders, etc. are another subject all together—and one well beyond what you'll ever find in this book.

Okay. Everything is apparently copasetic. It's just that the gun shoots better patterns than groups.

Is it a dog? A $700 tomato stake? That's possible. Just as Detroit turns its share of lemons disguised as vehicles, arms manufacturers and barrel makers do occasionally foul one off during mass production. And if it's a used gun—even one with a great track record—heaven only knows how it was used or cared for.

But, if we can adopt Perry Mason philosophy for use on ordnance, any gun should be considered innocent until proven guilty.

We've established that there's something wrong with our described rifle. Big wrong. The good news is that everything is correctible. You've got to find out just how simple or expensive the correction is going to be. So where do you start?

CLEAN THE BARREL FIRST

"The first thing we look at when someone brings us a sick rifle is the condition of the bore," says custom gunsmith Mark Bansner (261 East Main St., Adamstown, PA 19501. 215-484-2370). "A good 75 to 80 percent that we encounter have never been cleaned properly."

The gun has to be given a chance to perform, and it can't do that if it isn't properly cared for.

"Whether it's new or used, no rifle can shoot up to its potential if the bore isn't sanitary," says veteran benchrest shooter Joe Ventimiglia of Ohio. Be advised that Joe's knowledge and preoccupation with clean bores isn't just benchrest nitpicking. It also stems from his position as founder and president of Venco Industries, makers of Shooter's Choice gun care products.

"You've got to realize that primer, powder and lead or copper residue builds up with every shot. If it isn't cleaned out that residue will be ironed into a compound that's harder than the steel it forms on."

That explains why benchrest shooters spend more time cleaning than they do shooting.

"With that stuff in there, tolerances can change in as few as 15 or 20 shots. When the bullet no longer exactly fits the muzzle portion of the bore, accuracy is lost."

When the barrel is cleaned, conditioned and you're sure that the rifling is healthy, there's no embarrassment in taking a poor shooter to the gunsmith for an in-depth check-up. There is, afterall, no sense in you're treating headache symptoms when it might be cancer.

NOW LOOK FOR PROBLEMS

Besides, if the gun is as far off as in the opening scenario, chances are the problems can be rather easily detected by a practiced hand.

For instance, if the chamber isn't square to the bore, virtually all other moves are a waste of time. Or maybe it's a headspace problem, which may or may not be correctible with the current barrel.

Maybe it's something as simple as the wrong bullet for your particular rifling twist rate. Or the front screw on your scope base is too long and contacts the barrel. Hell, maybe the barrel isn't screwed in tightly.

"In diagnosing what's wrong with a sick rifle, it's really helpful if they can bring in some fired cases—they can tell you a lot of things right away," Bansner says.

"By reading the case you can tell if the striker is hitting the firing pin in the center. It'll tell you if the chamber is oversized or out of round and it can be an indicator of extreme headspace problems."

Factory cases are particularly helpful since the loads can be duplicated during testing. It gives the gunsmith a foundation and a known quantity to work from.

"We're always going to work factory loads through it to give us a basis to work from," Bansner says. "But if you have pretty good handloads, supply your gunsmith with some of those as well as some empty cases from them fired from that gun.

"He'll also need some pertinent information from those loads for testing."

A lot of accuracy problems are solved by correcting handloads or even switching brass.

"I'll never understand a guy getting a brand new .243 will trot out brass he'd used in his old .243," Bansner says. "The new chamber is bound to be much tighter. Give the gun a chance."

All used guns should probably have the crown polished while they're in the shop. That's just good insurance and a ragged crown might be one of several factors affecting accuracy.

You might also want to have your expert check bolt clearance. Bolt-barrel interference can string shots all over the place when the barrel heats up. If the rear guard screw is too long it can interfere with the bolt and striker, giving you light hits.

None of these factors alone are likely to result in four-inch groups—but cleaning them up certainly eliminates a variety of headaches that can add up to a big tumor.

Bansner also suggests adjusting the trigger so that it is crisp, with no creep.

"A good clean 2.5- to 3-pound trigger with no creep makes the gun easier and more comfortable to shoot and that alone can effect accuracy," Bansner notes.

Nothing swells tiny groups like an 8-pound trigger—unless, of course, you're the type who can crush cueballs in your fist.

Bansner also checks to see if the bolt face is square and laps in all the locking lugs for full contact. When you're dealing with 50,000 to 60,000 psi chamber pressure, sloppy fit can send performance south in a hurry.

"You strive for 100 percent contact, but you'll probably never get it," Bansner said. "Some factory guns come with only 30 or 40 percent contact, and that can definitely be improved. You need positive lock-up—you can't have it changing during the shot."

You might want to have your expert check firing pin protrusion (and retraction into bold body) and pin spring tension. While spring tension shouldn't be a problem in a recently manufactured gun, a 98 Mauser or match-grade '03 Springfield whose tack-driving reputation is slipping might have a tension problem.

CHECK THE ACTION-BARREL BEDDING

"Once the metal's taken care of, if the rifle still doesn't shoot, we look at the bedding," Bansner says. "If the metal is right but the

Adamstown, Pa., gunsmith Mark Bansner always asks shooters to bring fired cases with them to help in diagnosing a rifle's problems.

stock isn't then your rifle is not going to shoot—no matter what."

The action should rest solidly on two points with the barrel floating free of contact with the forearm. A pillar bedding job with either epoxy or aluminum pillars will help virtually any rifle solidify those two points where the action rests. This eliminates flexing the action or the stock so that puts pressure somewhere else.

"Factories like to put a third pressure point at the forearm tip of the stock," Bansner says. "That third point tends to dampen the vibrations in the barrel. But the only time I've found that to be effective is if you have a perfect barrel—the bore is perfectly concentric with the outside.

"The vast majority of barrels are not perfect. It doesn't mean that they're bad, but because they aren't perfect that third pressure point dampens the vibrations unevenly and differently every time.

"Free floating allows the barrel to do its own thing. When it's on its own you'll find barrel whip will be the same every shot with a particular load."

DON'T EXPECT TOO MUCH

Remember too that most factory rifles are not built to shoot minute-of-angle groups. In fact, until recently manufacturers would rather submit to nude public flogging than discuss the accuracy of their off-the-shelf rifles. The perfecting of the button-rifling process has improved barrel-to-barrel comparative accuracy, but most need some work. Some certainly do perform at MOA and many others have the potential, but a factory rifle right out of the box is built for the average hunter who is going to be shooting at a relatively large target inside 100 yards.

"That kind of accuracy is fine for the vast majority of shooters," Bansner says. "But generally if you want better performance than that, you'll have to take your gun to someone who specializes in custom shooting work."

Thus whether you've got a problem gun or a run-of-the-mill factory piece, it likely can be improved by a skilled and experienced hand.

"In rare cases after you go through all of the metal and stock work—after your basic Medicare for your rifle—there's still a chance that it may not shoot," Bansner warns.

"At that point it can only be a poor barrel—usually rifling that was cut poorly or inconsistent. Without a doubt a new barrel will correct the problem."

Virtually all shooting problems are solveable. It's just that the solutions range from cleaning a barrel to replacing it—and it takes a trained eye to know the answers.

Chapter 23
BIG BORE: Today's Shotgun Slugs & Barrels

Hunting deer with a shotgun has been likened to hitting a baseball with a broom handle. Either implement will get results, but neither would be the tool of choice.

With whitetails and humans enjoying population explosions in roughly the same areas, elbow room is at a premium. Millions of deer hunters in eastern and southern states are thus forced to go to bat with broom handles, so to speak.

The Foster-type slug is actually a die-punched cup of lead with thin skirts designed to flare and seal the bore.

The shotgun's limited range is the legal preference to the potential next-county lethality of the modern rifle.

In some areas buckshot is the only fodder allowed. But to most shotgun toters, deer hunting means using rifled slugs. While rifle hunting is preferable for obvious reasons, both buckshot and rifled slugs have their places.

Buckshot is the longstanding choice of southerners hunting over dogs in swamps and brush. And African white hunters preferred a big bore loaded with buckshot when entering the tall grass in search of wounded lions.

Shotguns loaded with slugs were the weapon of choice when tiger hunting was in its heyday in India, and in Vietnam more than one combat marine found a slug gun to be a welcome companion in up-close-and-personal confrontations.

Having grown up in the shotgun-only environs of New York's Southern Tier, I am well acquainted with the strengths and drawbacks of slug-shooting. A half-hour's ride east to the Catskills or south into Pennsylvania puts me in rifle country, so comparisons are easy to make.

Being of sound mind and body, I always preferred the

Today's slug guns and loads are capable of outstanding accuracy.

Rifling marks are shown in this comparison of fired and unfired sabot sleeve halves.

A representation of state-of-the-art slugs (L to R): Activ, Lightfield Hybred Sabot, Remington Copper Solid (sabot), conventional sabot (Winchester & Federal), Brenneke Golden Slug, conventional Foster-type slug (Winchester, Federal and Remington).

Due to the massive concussion and recoil of slug guns, good quality scopes and steel rings are a must.

Today's sabot selection, with and without sleeves (L to R): Lightfield Hybred, Remington Copper Solid, conventional (Winchester or Federal).

obvious advantage rifles represented. But in my youth opportunities were far more plentiful in shotgun country. Besides, having a different gun for small game than you did for deer was viewed by the elders as a symbol of conspicuous consumption.

Our bird and rabbit guns were transformed into deer guns merely by switching loads. It was common knowledge even then that open-choked guns threw slugs better than full-chokes, but other than that, there was very little theory involved.

After all, with only a single bead sight, we were pointing rather than aiming. Combine that with a trigger designed to be slapped rather than squeezed and accuracy was akin to hitting a pie plate two shots out of four at 50 yards.

The elders were resigned to such performance, the feeling being that we were asking shotguns to do things they simply were not designed to do.

The first true departure came when dad and the uncles agreed to buy all of our hunting party members Williams peepsights one Christmas. Their installation transformed our guns from pointers to aimers.

Next I began to experiment with various slugs rather than depend on the previous-year hand-me-downs inherited when dad bought his five new ones each fall.

More than a little experimentation unveiled a great deal to me about slug shooting. And I've been learning ever since.

TECHNOLOGY MAKES ITS MARK

Well skinny cigarettes for ladies ain't the only things that have come a long way, baby.

Over the last two decades, slug shooting has taken a quantum leap forward in both respectability and accuracy.

Technological advances in both barrels and projectiles has reshaped the whole idea of slug shooting. While rifles are still an obvious advantage, slug guns can no longer be described as weapons of last resort.

Today's serious slug shooter has a specialty gun—rifled barrel, scope, magnum recoil pad, maybe even a Monte Carlo stock.

They are, in effect, .72-caliber rifles. Two-season versatility is gone. These barrels have sniper-like potential at 100 yards with slugs but would spin a 2-ounce load of No. 6 shot in all directions at once.

In an area where 50-yard accuracy was once considered problematical at best, today's high-end commercial slug guns and loads will group two inches at 100 yards in expert hands.

In fact, if you want to push the envelope a bit, there are custom guns out there that have achieved repeated 100-yard groups inside a half-inch. Granted these are hand-built $1,500 guns in the hands of world-class benchrest shooters—but it gives you an idea of what can be done.

Slug barrel technology is relatively new. Ithaca Gun came out with the first true specialty gun in 1959 when it produced its venerable Model 37 pump in the Deerslayer version.

The gun featured a full cylinder 12-gauge smoothbore barrel—no forcing cone at the chamber or muzzle—in a .704-inch diameter. Most other 12-bores of the day miked in the .730-plus range.

Nobody laughed that the Deerslayer barrels came with rifle sights. But that was pretty much the extent of slug barrel development for a long time. The market was too small for the big manufacturers to get interested.

The next step came in the late 1970s when Olie Olson of E.R. Shaw barrels began wondering what it would take to make slugs shoot straighter.

His home was in Allegany County, Pa., a shotgun-only island in an ocean (more than a million deer hunters) of riflemen. The innovative gunsmith started rifling smoothbores to improve the performance of shotguns mandated for deer hunters in his area.

By the mid-1980s Shaw was marketing 12-gauge rifled barrel blanks to gunsmiths and was retrofitting their barrels to solid frame-style guns to which barrels could be permanently affixed. The list of suitable guns, however, was a short one.

About two years later the Hastings Corp. of Kansas started importing French-made rifled Paradox barrels to fit more popular brands.

In 1987, taking advantage of a liberalization of New York state hunting regulations, Ithaca Gun introduced the first commercial gun with a rifled barrel—its Model 87 Deerslayer II, complete with modified Monte Carlo stock and a receiver drilled and tapped for scope mounts.

Mossberg followed shortly there after with its rifled-barrel Model 500 Trophy Slugster pump. And U.S. Repeating Arms (Winchester) and Remington joined the rifled-barrel bandwagon in the 1990s.

In terms of autoloaders, Heckler & Koch of Virginia has been importing Italian-made Benelli autos and affixing Shaw barrels for quite a while.

Remington had the second rifled autoloader when it put a spiral tube on the 11-87 two years ago, in addition to a rifled Model 870 SPS pump. Winchester joined the rifled ranks in 1993.

Ithaca Gun is importing Fabarms' Ellegi autoloader, fitted with a 26-inch Paradox rifled bore. In 1993 Mossberg's Model 9200 is the latest American autoloader to be fitted with a rifled bore.

Thompson Center Arms and innovative New England Firearms (H&R 1871) both put out single-shot, rifled-barrel 12-gauges in the late 1980s. New England's version was the $125 Tracker, which has evolved into the 980 Slugster—the industry's first bull-barrelled slug gun. The 980 features a 10-gauge barrel blank drilled and rifled for a 12-gauge bore. The resulting thick-walled barrel and strong lock-up makes for outstanding accuracy. It remains to be seen how popular a 9-pound single-shot will become, even with a $200 price tag.

In 1994 Marlin came out with a rifled barrel version of its venerable Goose Gun and called it the 512 Slugmaster. Browning also has a bolt-action slug gun in the making and rumors have it that Savage will join the rifled barrel field soon.

SHOTGUN SLUGS COME OF AGE

Loads have come an even longer way. Until the 1930s slug shooters' only load was the pumpkin ball—a spherical ball of lead loosely loaded over cardboard wads. They were molded undersized to fit through any choke dimension and accuracy was laughable.

Shotguns in those days served as little more than modern muskets. Accuracy, needless to say, was less than desirable.

In 1931 Winchester-Western ballistician Karl M. Foster developed the projectile that is the basis of most American-made slugs today. The Foster slug was a soft piece of lead die-punched into a U-shaped cup. The rounded head of the hollow-based projectile was thicker than the sides, providing stability in flight, much as would a sock with a rock in the toe. The skirts of the cup were designed to expand and seal the bore.

They are called rifled slugs because of the "rifling grooves" or flutes swedged into the outside walls. While these grooves give the

Expansion and weight retention are the biggest advantages of the Foster-type slug.

impression that they give the slug rotation and therefore stability in flight, a ballistician once confided in me that their main purpose was to slightly reduce bearing surface and to give slugs a modicum of sales appeal.

The Foster slug has a highly inefficient shape, heavy weight and low velocity—but it stood as a vast improvement over pumpkin balls. They were an improvement over pumpkin balls and the basis for American slugs for the next 50 years. The load's accuracy was actually limited by the barrels and chokes.

The soft lead slug didn't fit most bores tightly and was prone to tip slightly as it exited the chamber and into the forcing cone. It was further deformed as it passed through the choke and what exited the muzzle had a ballistical mind of its own.

The Fosters were also undersized to fit all bores, regardless of make or choke constriction. For years the 12-gauge slugs varied from .695 to .715 or .720 for the equally varied dimensions of the 12-gauge shotgun bore.

In a rifle, slugs and bores are within a half-thousandth of an inch. Throw a .695 inch 12-gauge Remington slug down a .730 shotgun barrel and we're talking about a major league mismatch. Afterall, would you load a .243 cartridge in a .308 bore?

But in 1982 Winchester's Mike Jordan redesigned his company's Foster slugs to a .730 diameter with improved concentricity.

Federal followed in 1985, prompting Ithaca Gun to swell its .704 Deerslayer bore to the current .719 to avoid build-ups in barrel pressure. Remington finally expanded its Foster slugs to the industry standard in 1993.

Wilhelm Brenneke designed a slug in the 19th century, but it wasn't available on these shores until the late 1930s. Its big diameter, attached-wad design and longer bearing surface made the German-made slug a smoothbore favorite of more discriminating shooters.

Activ loaded the Italian-made Servo slug in its all-plastic hulls for years before designing its own load in 1992. The new load has better ballistics than anything on the market.

At about the time Olson was playing with the first rifled barrels in the very early 1980s Smith & Wesson was giving up rights to an experimental load developed for law enforcement use. The developer, Ballistic Research Industries of Soquel, Calif., reacquired the patent and tooling with the idea of marketing it to hunters.

Designed for police use to shoot through glass, doors, partition walls, car bodies and even engine blocks, the BRI sabot became a commercial sportsmen's load with a simple packaging change.

Patterned after long-range artillery loads, the sabot consisted of a .50-caliber wasp-waisted pellet encased in a two-part plastic sleeve. The sleeve fell off shortly after leaving the muzzle, sending the pellet—far more aerodynamic than conventional slugs—to fly down range.

The sabots were particularly accurate in rifled barrels since the rifling could take a good grip on the plastic sleeves, imparting a stabilizing spin on the bullet.

Winchester bought BRI's patent in 1990 and Federal redesigned the original (expired) BRI patent into its own version a year later.

Today both companies market two grades of sabots—Winchester the Standard Velocity and Supreme Hi-Impact loads and Federal the Classic and Supreme loadings.

Remington made the biggest stretch in slug shooting to date when it unveiled the Copper Solid Sabot in 1993. The .52-caliber hollow-point bullet is machined from copper bar stock, featuring a slight boattail. The nose is cross-cut to assure expansion—a factor that other saboted loads can't achieve on deer-sized game.

The Copper Solid's sabot is a one-piece, tenacle-grip affair similar to Remington's Accelerator rifle ammunition of the 1970s.

New for 1994, the Lightfield Hybred EXP Sabot has taken the industry by storm, not to mention surprise. A radical combination of sabot and attached-wad designs, the new slug shows accuracy rivaling other sabots but also carries a 1.25-ounce payload and expands beautifully. It's the first sabot to fill that bill. The Lightfield comes only in 2 3/4-inch 12-gauge right now.

Be advised that 3-inch loads, while ballistical giants on paper, are virtually always inferior in terms of accuracy. Most are simply the same projectile as their shorter cousins loaded over a larger powder charge and wad. They're built for marketing, not accuracy. The new technology is based primarily on 12-gauge 2 3/4-inch loads and it will probably take a while for the trickle-down to effect the other variants. In fact, custom slug guns come only with 2 3/4-inch chambers.

Remington, however, loads a totally new projectile in its 3-inch Copper Solid. This could be the first step in a true Magnum load worth shooting.

Some guns have faster rifling twist rates—Ithaca has an optional 1-turn-in-25 and the Benelli switched to 1-in-28 Shaw barrel in 1993, the same twist rate as the Marlin—which ballisticians say stabilizes saboted ammunition better than the 1-in-34 to 36 twists offered by the other brands.

One turn in 36 seems to handle Foster ammnunition best, according to research by Olson and Randy Fritz of Bloomsburg, Pa., the aforementioned benchrest champion and custom slug gun builder. One in 34 is a good compromise (Fosters or sabots).

All smoothbores with choke systems can be fitted with a screw-in rifled tube today. The results, however, are predictable when a full-bore slug reaches virtual terminal velocity before slamming into a short rifling segment. More deformation occurs than stabilization.

I've shot plenty of rifled chokes, but the longer (5-inches) external Browning tube is probably the best. None, however, are a match for a fully rifled bore, regardless of ammunition, but the Browning comes very close.

The most accurate slug guns will always be solid-frame style with screw-in barrels. If you're truly serious about reaching accuracy potential, have a gunsmith pin or at least Loctite your barrel in place.

Regardless of barrel configuration, no shotgun is going to reach its accuracy potential with a factory trigger. Shotgun triggers aren't designed to be squeezed.

Some slug gun makers endeavor to tighten and lighten triggers but most fail. One factory rep told me his company wanted all slug guns to go out at a maximum four-to-five pound pull.

When distributor complaints of heavy triggers came in, he checked the next gun off the assembly line and found a 12-pounder.

Virtually all production guns could use a trigger job, although you'll find the actual rate and degree of creep will vary from gun to gun on the shelf. My personal Ithaca Deerslayer II has had its trigger worked over by custom builder Mark Bansner of Adamstown, Pa.

The comb on a shotgun is also likely to be lower than you'd like for scope use. Ithaca uses a modified Monte Carlo stock, but I still augmented that with a strap-on leather comb pad popular with trapshooters. The Mossberg 500 comes with an adjustable add-on comb—by far the best idea among the test guns.

Consider that slug guns are pretty much limited to 120-yard shooting and shorter. Sabots show good ballistics out to 200 yards, but begin to tumble beyond 120–130 yards. Foster and other full-bore slugs simply can't be fully stabilized beyond 80 yards.

Therefore any scope stronger than four-power is a waste. In fact, two- and three-power scopes are plenty.

Use steel scope rings. Shotguns develop markedly less chamber pressure than rifles but their receivers are not designed to contain the concussion like a rifle. Sturdy rings and mounts are an absolute necessity on a slug gun.

Because of recoil, the concept of mounting the scope directly on the barrel or via a barrel-mounted cantilever system was once considered best for a shotgun.

Custom builders, however, find that for absolute best accuracy the mounts must be on the receiver. Beware of bolt-on side-saddle mounts. Because they distribute the concussion throughout their mass (like a cantilever), they have a tendency to move zero, regardless of how tightly they are installed.

I managed to tame that effect somewhat by caulking the inside of a B-Square mount bolted to the receiver of my personal Browning Auto-5.

Virtually all of the new technology is directed toward saboted slugs and rifled barrels. But that currently represents only about 10 percent of the market.

Part of the reason is cost—sabots often cost four to five times as much as conventional Foster slugs. Part is the vast number of smoothbore guns in circulation.

But a major factor has to be that despite the advances, the saboted ammunition—while slightly more accurate—is ballistically inferior to full-bore slugs inside of 75 yards. And surveys show that nearly 90 percent of all deer taken in shotgun territory are killed from 75 yards and closer.

The full-bore slugs—led by Activ—fly faster, hit harder, expand better and generate far more hydrastatic shock than the harder, smaller sabots at that distance.

Remington's Copper Solid is closing the gap, but the full-bore slugs still have a distinct advantage. Count the Lightfield among the full-bores even though it is technically a sabot.

For years the industry's minimum quoted standard for lethality on a whitetail was considered to be 1,200 foot pounds. Regardless of yardage, if your load retained that minimum it would anchor a whitetail.

That's a rather dubious figure when you consider that penetration is ruled so much by shot angle and location. If you put a hole through both lungs of any animal it's done—and it doesn't take 1,200 foot pounds to do that job.

In light of the nature of slugs and the recent advances, current industry insiders are putting that lethality figure at closer to 800 or 900 foot pounds for full-bore slugs and maybe even less for the harder sabots.

So check the tables. Your slug is a buck stopper at any distance where it's still stable and retains upwards of 900 foot pounds of energy.

Now it's up to you to shoot straight.

OPTICS & SIGHTS

Rifle sights are obviously much better than a single bead, and a peepsight makes the shooter be more disciplined, which usually means better accuracy.

But serious slug hunters today use low-power scopes. At 50 or 100 yards, you'll never be able to tell if the differences in barrels and/or loads is you or the implement unless you've got pinpoint optics.

To my way of thinking, anything stronger than 4X is overkill in slug-hunting, where the average shot is inside of 60 yards. I went from a peepsight on my smoothbore to a 4-power Leupold on the rifled barrel gun. The scope gives me a good field of view, plenty of magnification at any range out to 100 yards, and gathers light very well. For target shooting or accuracy testing I have a 3X9 Nikon.

Whatever power you select, make sure it is a good-quality scope. The inexpensive sorts shake apart quickly unde the high-concussion stress of shotgun recoil. Stick with steel rings and Locktite the mounting screws.

Many slug hunters prefer Quick-Point type sights, which provide no magnification, but center the target in a scope-like glass that has a flourescent dot fixed in the center for aiming purposes.

SUITABLE GAUGES

This is not to offend any small-bore aficianados, but 12-gauge is the level where the technological advances are being made.

Up until the 1960s the 16-gauge was a popular slug gun because of its speed and trajectory advantage over the only slightly more powerful 12-gauge.

But with the obsolescence of the 16-bore, the 12 stands virtually alone. Sure, plenty of deer are killed each year by 20-gauge slugs. But beyond 60 yards the extreme energy loss in most loads (there are exceptions) and subsequent drop in killing power of the 20-gauge slug make it a marginal choice. Slugs are also made in the .410 configuration, but are not even close to suitable for game larger than rodents and rabbits—even though it is ballistically superior to a .44 Magnum handgun.

Federal does make a 3.5-inch 10-gauge slug, but ballistics are close to that of its 3-inch 12-gauge slug and 10-gauge guns suitable for accurate slug shooting are few and far between.

In the ever-evolving world of slug shooting, one thing is clear—regardless of your gun-barrel preference, try all available types of ammunition to find what is best suited.

Of course, next year things might change, too. . . .

Buckshot is a very effective short-range load.

Chapter 24
Buckshot, an Alternative

There may be no more fearsome hand-carried weapon than a shotgun loaded with buckshot. And that statement has become even less arguable in the last 10 years.

It wouldn't be taking too much journalistic license to state that improvements in shotguns, slugs and buckshot loads have, in the last decade, outraced all other developments in the hunting arena.

We've looked at the development of the rifled slug, now let's look at its alternative—the buckshot load.

Development of the shot cup and granulated plastic buffering have turned the once willy-nilly patterning characteristics of buckshot into an even more devastating tool.

Previously, users of No. 00 (double-aught) buckshot found patterns extremely ragged at close range—to the point where a deer-sized target might be missed altogether at 40 yards.

The bigger the pellet (OO pellets are .33 caliber), you see, the more crowded they were in the bore. The majority of the pellets were damaged or worn by the barrel walls as they sorted themselves out en route to the muzzle.

Many buckshot hunters, in those days, opted for smaller shot such as No. 4 (.24 caliber), which patterned much denser than the larger shot. The lethality of No. 4 shot, however, is questionable beyond 20-30 yards.

Full choke was almost invariably the choice of old-time buckshot users. But today, with the plastic sleeves and buffer keeping the shot from being deformed in the barrel, good patterns can be obtained with modified or even improved cylinder choking.

New loads, including the relatively new No. OOO (.36 caliber pellets), are more effective than ever in open-choke guns, too, for the same reason.

With today's loads, effective ranges have lengthened appreciably. For instance, No. 00 today, fired through a full-choke 12-gauge barrel, would probably average 50 percent (six of 12 pellets) in the traditional patterning target of a 30-inch circle at 70 yards. Just 10 years ago a 50 percent pattern could be achieved at no longer than 40 yards.

But again, we're judging buckshot by old standards. A 30-inch pattern is a fine criteria for wingshooting birds, but we're aiming at 12- to 16-inch vital area in a deer. A pie plate is a better target.

In extended testing I've found No. 00 buck won't average more than eight of its pellets in a pie plate-sized target at 30 yards. With some choke constrictions I didn't even get four pellets in the target. Some loads liked full choke, others improved cylinder and I found that just a tiny change in constriction could make a dramatic difference in pattern density.

While growing up as a shotgun hunter for deer, slugs were the only legal fodder in my area and I've got to say that hindsight makes me glad of that fact. Buckshot loads might be better than ever but as far as I'm concerned anything beyond 30 yards is mighty chancey—and with some load-choke combinations 20 yards might be too far.

If you have to shoot buckshot, be sure to do your homework. Try a variety of shot sizes (No. 00 is probably the most versatile and effective) and a variety of chokes (extended chokes seem to outperform convention screw-ins) before making a decision. And remember when patterning that a 10-inch pie plate is a far better judge of buckshot effectiveness than the traditional 30-inch circle.

Buckshot comes in six sizes from No. 000 (10 pellets, .36 caliber in 3-inch shell), No. OO (15 pellets, .33 caliber in 3-inch and 12 pellets in 2.75-inch shell), No. 0 (12 pellets, .32 caliber in 2.75 inch shell), No. 1 (20 pellets, .30 caliber in 2.75-inch shell, 24 in 3-inch shell) and No. 4 (41 pellets, .24 caliber in 3-inch shell, 34 pellets in 2.75-inch). The number of pellets may vary with manufacturer.

American manufacturers usually reserve No. 2 and No. 3 shot for 20-gauge loads.

BUCKSHOT STATE-BY-STATE

BUCKSHOT ALLOWED	NOW ALLOWED
Alabama (dog hunting only)	Arizona
Alaska	Colorado
Arkansas (specific areas)	Connecticut
California (specific areas)	Illinois
Delaware	Indiana
Florida	Iowa
Georgia (specific areas)	Kansas
Hawaii	Kentucky
Idaho	Minnesota
Louisiana	Missouri
Maine	Nebraska
Maryland (specific areas)	Nevada
Massachusetts (specific areas)	New Mexico
Michigan (specific areas)	New York
Mississippi	North Dakota
Montana	Ohio
New Hampshire (specific areas)	Oklahoma
New Jersey	West Virginia
North Carolina	Wisconsin
Oregon	Wyoming
Pennsylvania (specific areas)	
Tennessee (specific areas)	
Rhode Island	
South Carolina	
Texas	
Utah	
Vermont	
Virginia	
Washington	

CANADA

British Columbia	Manitoba
Quebec	Nova Scotia
	Saskatchewan

The MK-85 Knight Hawk by Modern Muzzleloading is an example of how far blackpowder rifles have advanced.

<u>Chapter 25</u>
Blackpowder Hunting:
A Different Experience

Powder, ball, cap. That's the simple yet absolutely essential chronology for the successful operation of a blackpowder rifle.

One would think that a reasonably intelligent adult, particularly one who makes his living dealing with firearms, could handle such a simple scenario. Yes, one would think that, but the suddenly-wiser 6-point buck bounding away from my treestand through the North Carolina underbrush is living, breathing proof that I've screwed up the equation somewhere.

The loud snap in place of the expected "kaboom!" leads one to believe that perhaps I've skipped a step—like the powder.

A missed opportunity is discouraging enough. Particularly one botched by stupidity. But added to it is the certain knowledge that the little misadventure is going to result in the shortening of my shirt tail and a fusillade of humiliating prattle. This quaint southern ritual is gleefully carried out by host Edwin "Booger" Harris on those who fail to convert deer into venison under his guidance.

No alibis are accepted in the ever-playful environment of Harris' Pungo Acres Hunting Retreat, a comfy little camp situated near the eastern North Carolina village of Pantego. Nobody is exempt from Booger's constant banter nor humbling garment mutilation especially not "Yankee spoatsratters."

There are special blackpowder hunting seasons in 48 states.

Regulations for blackpowder hunting vary from state-to-state.

"Ah don't know 'bout where y'all come from," says Booger, an ever-widening mischievous grin splitting his ruddy face. "But down here when ya'll pull the trigger and the deer runs off not hurt, we call that a miss!"

Sure it's arguable whether my aforementioned misfortune should be classified as a "miss" on technical grounds. But I must admit that there were a few other miscues—ranging from premature ignition to hangfire to a flat-out miss—over the course of my week at Pungo Acres that fully justified a ragged strip of Tru-Leaf with my name on it tacked to "Booger's Wall of Fame."

Blackpowder hunters must accept missing as part of the experience. So is the frustration of not being able to follow up with another shot on demand. To many folks those are also the attractions to primitive weaponry, not to mention the extended seasons.

Every state except Montana and Georgia has a special black powder season and muzzleloaders are legal in all states during the firearms deer season. No wonder the legions of charcoal burners is growing every year. Some states mandate actual "primitive weaponry" (Pennsylvania allows only flintlocks), but most are far more liberal with their regulations on muzzleloaders. Because of that, technology is running rampant in the muzzleloader arena. Today's in-line blackpowder guns are commonly mounted with scopes and can be every bit as accurate as a centerfire rifle out to 200 yards and still pack sufficient punch to turn the lights out on a whitetail beyond that distance.

Gonic Muzzleloaders of New Hampshire, for instance, makes a magnum rifle that accepts more than 200 grains of powder and has been used on thick-skinned African game and big bears.

As I said muzzleloaders are fun but I'm no expert. I've got one because it extended my opportunities in the deer woods—the same reason I took up bowhunting. If they opened a special spear-hunting deer season I'd probably apply.

No, I'm not a muzzleloader aficionado. No fringed buckskin or elaborate possibles bag here. No scopes or in-line systems. A couple of ramrod tools in a Zip-Loc bag in one pocket of a Tru-Leaf jacket, four Quick Shots holding premeasured loads in another pocket, capper on a lanyard with the grunt tube and it's showtime.

Unlike many states, North Carolina's blackpowder regulations are very liberal—sort of a shoot-what-ya-brung attitude that allows in-line guns, scopes, any type ball or bullet. My rather austere choice of ordnance started life as a .54-caliber CVA Mountain Rifle kit more than a dozen years ago. The barrel has been glass-bedded, the sights altered, a Mountain States Super Rod replaced the original and the trigger is set at whisper weight for offhand target shooting.

We had shooting opportunities all six days while hunting Harris' 8,000-acre lease and areas on the adjacent Pungo River Unit of the Pocosin Lakes federal wildlife refuge. Despite several botched opportunities (remember, that's part of the fun), my

A Kap Kover is a must for keeping percussion nipples and caps dry in inclement weather.

venerable front-stuffer managed to fill three whitetail tags at Pungo Acres. The statewide limit for deer is five, at least one of which must be antlerless. There are some areas where a late-season bonus antlerless tag inflates the bag to six.

"Don't expect no record-book racks down here," Booger noted when I booked the Pungo Acres hunt the previous spring. "We got quantity, not a whole lot of quality. The average deer taken here ain't but 95 pounds but ya'll can take two a day. That's if ya'll can shoot straight."

But you can't tell that to Thurman Smith of Seagrove, NC, a longtime Pungo client. During our visit Smith limited out on bucks, including a 202-pound 8-pointer that Booger was quick to point out as an exception rather than the rule. Nevertheless, my brother-in-law, Dean Sunderland took a 7-pointer that weighed 157 pounds and all three of the small-racked bucks that I tagged were heavier than 130. Even Booger took time to tag a 165-pound buck with curved unique 13-inch spikes.

North Carolina is divided into four geographical regions for deer hunting from the the coastal flats to the western mountains. The Eastern region hosts the earliest muzzleloader and regular firearms seasons, both starting in October while the other three regions don't open until November. Antlerless deer restrictions vary by region and often by county. No less than four counties intersect in Pungo Acre's hunting area.

Booger's down home playful personality is a big part of Pungo Acres' appeal. The stocky, barrel-chested Tar Heel wears his red neck heritage like a badge and delights in north-south banter with visiting Yankee hunters. Those seeking the bourbon-by-the-hearth style Southern hunting lodge should keep on looking. Pungo Acres is more hunting camp than lodge as its low prices and playful atmosphere attest.

Muzzleloader season in many states precedes the regular firearms season and thus finds milder, but often more humid or damp weather. And nothing bothers a muzzleloader more than dampness. Black-powder is extremely hygroscopic (attracts moisture from the air) and water, of course, destroys the mixture's volatility. No boom.

North Carolina's coastal plain in October is, as one might imagine, damp. Dean and I used Kap Kovers to seal the nipples and most of the other guys used latex muzzle covers to seal out dampness. There are plenty of substitutes to seal the muzzle but I've never been able to explain to my wife why I needed to take condoms on a hunting trip—so I tape the muzzle.

On the final day of our hunt I left a deep-woods stand early to still-hunt my way in the rain back to the roadside croplands in that magic time just before dusk.

My mind was replaying highlights of the previous five days when I came to high reeds flanking a drainage ditch. Peering through the head-high reeds I could make out a small rack about 60 yards on the other side.

Slowly ducking, I removed the Kap Kover from the nipple and took two steps sideways to afford myself a shooting line other than the way the buck was looking. I straightened, found the base of the young buck's neck in the sight picture, set the trigger and touched one off, almost in one motion.

Through the smoke I could see clods of dirt flying from a trail-side myrtlewood bush as the buck's hooves desperately sought traction in the thick vegetation. Suddenly everything was still.

Crawling through the short patch of brush I found the neck-shot buck lying dead 15 yards from where he'd been hit.

A fitting end to a memorable hunt—and one that I look forward to doing again.

*   *   *   *

Pungo Acres Hunting Retreat may be contacted at PO Box 55, Pantego, NC 27860 or by calling (919) 935-5415.

BASICS OF BLACKPOWDER

Blackpowder is the older, slower-burning, dirtier brother of modern smokeless powder.

Yes, they're related but the two should never be used interchangeably because of their vastly different properties.

Blackpowder is far more volatile than smokeless powder and must be handled very carefully. By the same token, never use smokeless powder in a muzzleloader. Black powder guns are made of low carbon steel that will not withstand the high pressures of smokeless powder. Smokeless powders can cause muzzleloading barrels or breeches to rupture or blow-up.

Blackpowder comes 7,000 grains to the pound and can be found in four different granulations—each of which has its own use.

The largest granular size in black powder is called FG and is used in large shotguns, muskets and small cannons. The next size, FFG, is suggested for use in rifles of .50 caliber or larger as well as shotguns.

FFFG is the smallest size suggested for use as a propellent and is commonly used in rifles under .45 caliber as well as pistols and revolvers. FFFFG is used only as a priming powder in flintlock guns.

VELOCITY IS A KEY FOR BLACK POWDER HUNTING

Velocity is twice as important as bullet weight in the formula to determine bullet energy. That's why smaller, higher-velocity centerfire loads are generally more lethal than muzzleloader projectiles.

But there are other considerations that make muzzleloaders good hunting tools. Being heavier, the muzzleloader ball has more momentum for better penetration. If the projectile has sufficient speed at impact to deform itself, the heavier bullet produces a much more profound wound.

The minimum velocity at the point of impact that will provide adequate deformation of a round ball is 1,250 feet per second. At less than 1,150 feet per second the ball will not deform and will simply punch a small hole through the target or animal.

One of the biggest enemies of velocity is a dirty bore. The ball must have a clear, clean path in order for the powder charge to be its most effective.

Traditional wisdom called for cleaning blackpowder firearms

with hot water. The thought was that hot water cleaned more thoroughly and evaporated quickly. Recent research has shown, however, that hot water may actually encourage corrision under some conditions.

Despite some high-tech product claims, blackpowder guns should be cleaned after every use. World class marksman swab the bore with solvent after every shot.

BLACKPOWDER RESIDUE MORE THAN ANNOYING

Blackpowder residue is messy stuff. A large quantity of solid residue generated when powder burns is black, sooty and clings to everything it touches.

More than half of a blackpowder charge's volume remains behind as ash and other residue after firing. Not only is it messy, but it accumulates so quickly that after just a few shots it cuts patches, deforms balls, causes misfires and hangfires and tightens the bore to the point it can become difficult to reload.

But those inconveniences and shooting impediments aren't the worst effect of blackpowder fouling. Worse yet, if allowed to collect, more and more residue will find its way to lock parts, in the bolster, nipple and on the clean-out screw. Because blackpowder is hygroscopic—it attracts moisture from the air rapidly—it is very corrosive. Thus fouling can cause springs and screws to rust through or a bolster or nipple to blow out of its seat as a shot is fired.

If enough shots are fired through an unclean bore that ash and residue can work down between the stock and barrel, causing massive rusting and rotting of the wood. It can creep into a minute metal flaw, suck moisture from the air and eventually rust a hole through the barrel.

DO's AND DON'Ts FOR BLACKPOWDER SHOOTERS

Blackpowder shooting enjoyed a renaissance with the country's bicentennial in 1976 and the sport has blossomed ever since. With the equipment now more available and affordable than ever, many people are being drawn to blackpowder shooting who may not be well-versed in the sport.

Here is a list of Blackpowder Do's and Don'ts gleaned from interviews with a variety of muzzleloading experts:

* Do ram the ball until it's seated on the charge before attempting to shoot again after a shot failed to clear the barrel.

* Do wait at least a minute after a misfire before examining the gun to be sure that a latent spark is not active.
* Don't permit your blackpowder gun to remain in hot sunlight between shots. The barrel will heat unevenly, causing non-uniform expansion and will kill accuracy.
* Don't place your finger on the muzzle or barrel while examining a blackpowder gun. Perspiration contains acids and salts that cause rust to form rapidly.
* Do store blackpowder guns in areas that are dry. Avoid unlined canvas cases that can deface the finish.
* Don't use conventional bore cleaner. Blackpowder has entirely different characteristics than smokeless powder and must be treated accordingly. Use a specifically designed blackpowder bore cleaner.
* Don't prime the pan of a flintlock or cap a percussion gun until it is pointed at the target you intend to shoot.
* Do check the bore for oil before pouring powder for that first charge. Clean it first with a patch or two of solvent, then snap a cap or two to burn oil and gel out of the tube.

BLACKPOWDER REGULATIONS STATE-BY-STATE

Special Blackpowder seasons: Every state except Georgia and Montana.

Percussion actions legal: Every state except Pennsylvania

Metallic sights (peep) legal: Every state except Pennsylvania.

Telescopic sights legal: Arizona, Delaware, Florida, Illinois, Indiana, Iowa, Kentucky, Louisiana, Maine, Maryland, Michigan, Montana, New Hampshire, North Carolina, Ohio, South Dakota, Tennessee, Texas, Vermont, Wyoming.

Roundball legal: All states.

Conical bullet legal: All but Connecticut, New York and Pennsylvania.

Saboted bullets legal: All but Colorado, Massachusetts, New York, Pennsylvania, Rhode Island.

In-line ignition legal: All states except Pennsylvania.

Closed breach legal: All states except Kentucky, Michigan, Nevada, Oregon, Pennsylvania and Washington.

Information (1994) courtesy of International Blackpowder Hunting Association, PO Box 1180, Glenrock, Wyoming 82637.

Chapter 26
Bowhunting: Are Speed and Quiet Overrated?

He's gone now, but my friend Norm was once the most enthusiastic and opinionated bowhunters I've ever known. There are those who would charge that "enthusiastic and opinionated bowhunter" is a redundancy.

At any rate when Norm believed something he was passionate about it. He'd graduated with the rest of us from recurve to compounds, but his passion took him beyond us all. He literally wore out the eccentric wheels on a couple of compounds. And with them went his desire for the newfangled **wheel bows**.

Back to recurves. Recurves are what archery is supposed to be about, Norm preached. And they perform every bit as well as compounds—there never was any reason to change.

I beg your pardon? Norm, there's no comparison; compounds are much more efficient.

Norm and I were at a bow festival in Pennsylvania in the early 1980s when we came across a booth featuring an electronic trap that read arrow speed and energy.

This was it. The perfect argument ender.

Norm was shooting a 65-pound Bear takedown recurve

ED ASWAD PHOTO

The advent of the compound bow and aluminum arrows revolutionized shooting in the 1970s and brought thousands more people into the sport.

ED ASWAD PHOTO

and I cranked my Jennings compound to 65 pounds. His arrow was timed at 169 fps and 35 foot pounds of energy. I nocked the same arrow and released. Mine read 212 fps and 62 pounds.

The archery industry was revolutionized in the 1970s with the introduction of the compound bow. The next stage of progress was marked by the development of the programmed cam bow in the 1980s. Late in the decade low-stretch or no-stretch bowstring has fanned the flames a bit more.

ARROW SPEED SELLS

Where once you cast an arrow on an arching trajectory toward a target, now you can only track them by their vapor trails. Each advancement in technology added to just one factor in archery— arrow speed.

Speed sells, so that's where the technology was focused.

NOISE IS A FACTOR

But there are trade-offs in virtually all areas. In archery more speed is attained at the expense of quiet.

To a tournament archer, bow noise means little. But to a bowhunter stealth is everything. The concealment of form, smell and noise is deemed paramount.

And fast bows, particularly those with these new strings, are noisy suckers.

Like most bowhunters, I was long concerned with the quietness of my bow. Performance came first, but I was willing to lose a few feet per second to quiet my hunting implement.

But even when my bow was extremely quiet—by human standards—I'd had deer duck my arrow. Jumping the string it's called and it is as incredible to see as it is frustrating.

But I've also killed and missed deer that made no reaction to the sound of the bow.

The personal conclusion is that at the ranges eastern bowhunters shoot—typically inside 25 yards—a deer will react just as quickly to fffft! as it will to THWACK!!!!

"No matter what kind of bow you're shooting it's going to make noise that a deer can hear," said Dave Burnham, an archery design engineer in Syracuse, NY.

"And personally I don't think that noise itself matters."

Burnham and some other members of the Oneida Labs staff did a little informal field research during the 1988 bow season. Hunting for bucks, they purposely shot over the backs of any unspooked does that wandered into range.

"In each instance the arrow was past them before they reacted to the noise," Burnham said.

"To my way of thinking the attitude of the animal at the time of the shot is the difference. If that animal is spooky—if it's just been shot at before or chased out of its bed or something—then it will react much more quickly.

"If a spooked animal wants to jump the string no bow made is fast enough."

While hunting in Texas in January 1989 I was exposed to more than a dozen expert bowhunters. Their theories on noise were basically the same but their outlooks differed.

"On short shots I don't think noise is really a factor if the animal doesn't know you're there," said Chuck Ballweg, a professional arch er from northern California. "But when I'm hunting in the mountains where 60 and 80-yard shots are pretty common, it can be a factor."

Ballweg feels that long yardage gives the animal an opportunity to pinpoint the noise, notice the arrow in flight and react. He cited an antelope hunt in Africa where the skittish animals are notorious for jumping the string.

Nevertheless there are few us, regardless of of conviction, who go afield without some sort of noise-dampening device on the string.

"Regardless of what I think, we're in the business of selling bows," Burnham said. "And that means that I've got to design a quiet bow."

Informal research at Burnham's lab showed that puffs or cat-whiskers and brush buttons dampen the string noise by about two decibels. Whatever that means.

QUIET EFFECTS SPEED

That same research shows that arrow flight is slowed by about one foot per second for every five grains of weight increase. Thus an 87-grain puffs can slow the arrow flight by 17 feet per second—an unconscionable loss by today's standards.

"We see it all the time," Burnham said. "Somebody will call the factory and say he or she isn't getting within 30 feet per second of our advertised speed. We ask them to bring the bow in for a free check-up.

"Invariably the bow comes in with everything but the cat hanging on the string."

Anything attached to the string will slow it. It's like adding weight to the arrow. A no-stretch string is more susceptible than the old B-50 dacron types, but all are slowed by the various silencing and sighting apparatus.

Today's broadheads often feature replaceable pre-sharpened stainless steel blades.

Research shows that the closer the attachment is made to the nocking point (spot where the arrow hooks onto the string) the more it will slow the string. Consider that catwhiskers weigh 51 grains and puffs can be as much as 87 grains. A lot of speed is sacrificed in the name of lessened audio impact.

But how important is speed? It flattens trajectory so that the archer doesn't need to be as precise in his or her estimation of range. And a hunting arrow hits marginally harder at faster speeds.

The overdraw concept, which allows the archer to shoot a shorter and therefore lighter and faster arrow, is great for the field archer shooting distances of 40 or more yards.

But many experts see the overdraw as a disadvantage in hunting situations. Granted, the superior speed does eliminate some guesswork on yardages for the bowhunter. But the use of a lighter arrow means a loss of energy upon impact. While arrow energy is not a prime factor as it is with bullets, it can affect penetration. More energy is definitely better than less if the angle of penetration is severe or if the arrow hits resistance, such as heavy fur or a rib or bone.

Speed and noise are definitely factors for bowhunters. Selection boils down to personal preference—a decision based on knowledge of the entire situation.

"Poets sing and hunters scale the mountains primarily for one and the same reason—the thrill to beauty. Critics write and hunters outwit their game for one and the same reason—to reduce that beauty to possession."
—Aldo Leopold

PART VI:

ISSUES INVOLVED IN DEER HUNTING

"Any thought of first aid is immediately dismissed. There is no circumvention, no escape from this, the ultimate hunters' nightmare."

Chapter 27
Deadly Perception

Dawn is a still a pink hint in the eastern treetops when the coffee in the travel mug is finished off and it's time to get the gun and backpack out of the back seat.

Making the way down the familiar old skid trail into the lower hardwoods is a comfortable feeling, engendering memories of past quests and success.

After five minutes of walking it's still difficult to make out traditional landmarks. The stand is close, but exact location can't be determined until the fledging dawn relinquishes a few more hints.

Expectation is high. a sense of anticipation and confidence borne of familiar venue is rising with the new sun. This is the magical time one looks forward to each year.

A check of the watch confirms that it's almost legal shooting time, even though the heavy overcast is limiting the light. Nothing to do but wait.

A familiar feeling of reverence grows in the silent beauty of the sleeping woodlot. The quiet is pervasive. Peaceful. Calming.

What was that? A tick of alien sound profanes heavy silence, shaking the gentle lassitude. There it is again.

Over there—an almost imperceptible blur of movement and dark, indefinable color moves along a brushy edge. Where's the wind? Freeze. Just move the eyes. Slowly.

There it is, materializing out as it has so many times before out of the play of shadows in the dimly lit woodlot. The throat patch, the ears, the lowered head. The rack is there but indistinct against the brushy background. Any rack is acceptable when you've only got weekends to hunt.

It's a familiar scene. A much anticipated scene. Everything becomes almost mechanical.

The stock slides to the familiar spot on the cheek. The sights line

When the excitement of the hunt turns to horror . . .

A phenomenon known as Visual Closure occurs when you see part of what you think is a familiar object and your mind fills in the rest of the picture.

up behind the deer's shoulder. The safety eases off silently with a practiced move of the forefinger.

The finger gradually tightens on the trigger, confident in the knowledge of exactly where the sear will disengage.

Boom!

A familiar ringing in the ears is the only sound in the still hushed woodlot. The deer is gone. It must be down.

The shot was a good one, the feeling a curious mix of excitement, satisfaction and a certain sadness and finality that it's all over for another season.

The confident walk is short; maybe 75 yards, looking for the telltale horizontal white belly contrasting with the dimly lit forest floor.

But confidence turns immediately to horror.

Where the deer should be a man is sprawled on his back, legs and arms grotesquely askew like a crumpled puppet. Vacant eyes bulge skyward, the facial features contorted in death. Steam rises from terrible hole in his chest.

Any thought of first aid is immediately dismissed. There is no circumvention, no escape from this, the ultimate hunters' nightmare.

The scenario is fictional but similar incidents occur regularly every season. Too regularly.

IT'LL NEVER HAPPEN TO ME

We all think of mistaking another hunter for game as inconceivable—until we are shaken by experience. Hopefully our experience will not have lethal consequences.

The big game hunter often works in the world psychological researchers refer to as "early blur". His is the first pale hour of dawn in the woods and the last blue-gray wash of gathering twilight. Even at midday the sun-and-shadow dapple of the forest floor and broken shadows of the swamp can confuse vision.

Who among us hasn't stalked a "deer" that turned out to be a strange-shaped stump or the silhouette of a bush against the sky?

Tell me you've never turned a rustling leaf into a buck's ear, a horizontal patch of gray or brown into a flank, or a twisted maple branch into antlers.

The described phenomenon is, in fact, quite common. The technical term is "visual closure." The Dictionary of Visual Science defines it as "A perception of a single larger unit rather than a number of apparently unrelated parts. Also called collective configuration."

It's actually more of a psychological than visual phenomenon.

"Whats happens, in plain terms," explains Dr. Stephen Solomon, an optometrist, vision expert and hunter from Owego, New York, "is when you see part of an object—usually an object you are familiar with or trained to see—you see part of it and the mind literally fills in the rest of the picture.

"A hunter looking for deer or turkeys trains his eyes. And the anticipation makes it possible for his eyes to create a deer or turkey from branches, bushes, bark—just about anything under the right circumstances."

It's a sobering realization that, given a reasonably well-defined combination of normal physical and mental factors, any intelligent human being—expert or novice, man or woman, careless or responsible—can see a deer where no deer exists.

Until about 40 years ago the perfectly normal mental and physical combination of circumstances that occasionally led one hunter to kill another was a total mystery.

But in the mid-1950s Dr. Leonard Mead, a professor of psychology at Tufts University, began exploring the possibility that people have the ability to "see" objects they want to see.

Dr. Mead cited experiments that seemed to prove that any normal person, under certain conditions, is subject to a strange variety of wide-awake hallucination. He surmised that it was entirely within the realm of possibility for an eager hunter to conjure up a deer out of the play of light and shadow in the woodland.

TRUE AND TRAGIC STORIES

Most of us have experienced the phenomenon in a harmless situation. But it can, and all too often does, result in tragedy. Witness:

* A young mother is fatally wounded while standing in the backyard of her suburban home in Maine, less than 40 feet from her back door.

    The shooter, a hunter of 17 years experience, swears in court that he was shooting at a deer he was following in his scope. The fatal shot was fired at a distance of 60 yards. Investigators found no deer tracks. The woman was wearing white gloves and a blue coat.
* An upstate New York hunter, still-hunting in a light fog, spots a deer, takes a steady rest and shoots. The shotgun slug strikes a 75-year-old hunter in the face at a distance that investigators would later list as 62 feet. He died en route to the hospital.

    The shooter, an experienced hunter and church and community leader, is charged with second degree manslaughter.

He swears in court that he positively identified a deer as his target. The victim, who was seated on a log, was dressed in red-black plaid coat and was wearing a red baseball cap bearing "Bud" in white lettering across the crown.

* Two Quebec game wardens are crouched in a woods trail in anticipation of apprehending two poaching suspects just before dawn.

Before they can spring the surprise one of the suspects fires his crossbow while screaming "bear!" The bolt strikes one of the officers in the chest at a distance of nine yards, killing him.

The suspect swears in court that he had definitely identified the form in the trail as a bear.

* Another hunter in a northeastern state, standing with two members of his party at dusk, spots a deer crossing a fence on the skyline.

He remarks that it was still light enough to shoot, takes aim and fires. What had been perceived as a deer jumping a fence was, in fact, the shooter's 18-year-old son. The shot strikes the young man in the head, killing him instantly.

The shooter sends his colleagues for help, lays down next to his son's body and ends his own life.

In each of the aforementioned cases the shooter was an experienced hunter (each with at least 15 years of hunting) who had enjoyed regular success in deer seasons. Each shooter had passed hunter safety courses. Each was hunting in familiar territory.

PHENOMENON IN COURT

Not all hunting fatalities are prosecuted. But when they are, the phenomenon of visual closure is often incorporated in defense of the shooter.

In one case a 29-year-old New Hampshire hunter, on property familiar to him and supposedly off-limits to all other hunters, told his story in a police statement: "I had been the woods about two hours, during which time I had not seen any other hunters or heard any activity, such as shots, etc. I heard a noise on a bank across the gulley . . . that I thought was something walking."

The statement said he then studied the area and described seeing movement of a dark object that he identified as a deer. "I then looked through my rifle's scope and observed what I determined to be a deer and fired at the deer. Just after the shot I heard a man scream and a boy screamed and I screamed. I went to the area and tried to aid the man."

The victim, dressed in a red plaid shirt and green plaid vest and pants, was shot through the hip at a distance of less than 80 yards. He died in the woods.

The shooter's lawyer stated in a letter that his client ". . . believed firmly (then and now) that he had in fact seen a deer and shot at one. His convictions were so strong that I actually took a trained woodsman into the area to see if there were any deer tracks adjacent to where the victim was shot. Unfortunately, there were none."

The lawyer also enlisted the expert testimony of psychologist Dr. George Wolford of Dartmouth College, whose area of expertise is perception psychology.

The lawyer's letter says, "Dr. Wolford endorses the concept that individuals 'fill in' hazily seen objects with images drawn from their memory bank. His opinion is (the shooter) had a strong expectation of seeing a deer at the moment in question, and, therefore, in all probability did see a deer."

NO ONE IS IMMUNE

It's a sobering thought that no one is immune to this tragic phenomenon in the woods.

In fact, the more experienced the deer hunter—the more deer you've seen in the woods over the years—the more knowledge is stored in those memory banks. And the more likely you are to be tricked by your "mind's eye."

So what does the responsible sportsmen do to defend against falling victim to this psychological phenomenon?

Encouraging everyone to wear fluorescent or Blaze Orange (TM of Day-Glo Corp., Cleveland, OH) can go a long way toward alleviating this potential horror.

Studies have shown that the illusion can be blocked by something unnatural—such as an unusual color that would ruin the mind's initial hypothesis.

In the early 1960s two research psychologists from Harvard University's Center for Cognitive Studies, Dr. Jerome Bruner and

Dr. Mary Potter, studied perception. Their studies included the ability of the human eye to recognize various objects.

"Perception itself," Dr. Bruner wrote in the Harvard Alumni Bulletin of November, 1963, "is a magnificent achievement and yet, withal, visual perception is extraordinarily stupid."

Studying subtleties of perception, the researchers rigged a slide projector and displayed transparencies on a screen. The first picture subjects saw was hopelessly blurred. Then, over a period of two minutes, the image was gradually brought into sharp focus. The observers were asked to identify the picture as soon as they recognized it.

The researchers noted that recognition by the group came well past the point when anyone walking into the room would effect immediate recognition.

"There was something about living in early blur with the picture that prevented ready recognition of it," Dr. Bruner wrote.

Another interesting finding was that some of the observers suffered a form of hallucination in which they "recognized" the picture before it became clear, then continued to "see" that which their minds had willed them to see, even after full focus had been attained.

Jack Woolner, a former New Hampshire Fisheries & Game Department spokesman and outdoor writer, met with Bruner and Potter to discuss how their findings might effect hunters.

"They said that a hunter, given visual and/or sound clues of an animal such as a deer, could supply the missing parts form his memory bank and could see a deer where none existed." said Woolner, one of the pioneers of the use of fluorescent orange clothing for hunters.

"In turn, an unnatural bright color, such as fluorescent orange, would shatter such an illusion because it would cause the brain to report 'tilt' and recycle immediately. An unnatural bright color would be rejected in the assembling of the mental jig-saw puzzle of a deer."

Hypothesis? No, Woolner says; it's fact. Fluorescent orange shatters a dangerous illusion before it can take shape. The color is so startlingly vivid that it dispels all "deer clues."

Maybe you're the type who is willing to "take your chances" in the deer woods without Blaze Orange. That's up to you, but consider that in doing so you may well be potentially ruining the life of a fellow hunter who could, through no fault of his own, fall victim to the psychological phenomenon that could change both of your lives forever.

Chapter 28
The Story of Blaze Orange

A rustle in the brush to the left of the logging road snatches the hunter from a state of listless day-dreaming and causes him to drop to one knee in anticipation.

There it is again. Gun quickly to the shoulder, he peers over the sights for that expected first glimpse of brown. If it steps out on the logging road there isn't going to be much time to evaluate and shoot.

With both buck and antlerless tags tucked in a coat pocket and a vacant spot in the freezer, he's not going to be too choosy. But he will have to be quick.

The foreleg appears first, then a nose scouring the wintergreen that carpets the old woodland road.

Another step reveals the shoulder of the young forkhorn, setting off an internal signal. All systems go. Everything is automatic, as it's been so many times before. Cheek firmly to the familiar position on the stock; line up the sights; ease off the safety and squeeze the trigger.

Whoa! Stop!

Something interrupts. Something alien invades the sight picture, breaking the concentration. As the young buck browses mindlessly 40 yards away a movement beyond him has caught the hunter's eye.

Its brightness, the very nature of the object, tells the story immediately. It's his hunting partner, coming over the crest and down the logging road from the other direction.

Unknowingly he's stepped into the prospective line of fire. The sight of his fluorescent orange hat narrowly avoided a potential disaster.

Forty states and five Canadian provinces mandate the use of fluorescent orange clothing for big game hunting. The other 10 states strongly recommend its use.

ANOTHER DAY

On another day, in another woods, a hunter cautiously picks his way along a familiar route through the pre-dawn dimness to his stand. About 100 yards short of his destination he can discern a man—another hunter—leaning against a tree.

As he approaches it's obvious that the stranger is shaken. His skin is pale, eyes wide, his face drawn and distraught. His hands are shaking and his rifle lies in the leaves at his feet.

"I heard you over there, then could see the movement," he says in

Regulations vary state-to-state as to how much orange is mandatory and in what configuration.

a shaky voice. "I was convinced you were a deer. Absolutely convinced. I almost shot before I saw your orange vest.

"I could have killed you."

Both of these were personal experiences. But I'll bet that virtually every experienced hunter reading this has encountered or knows someone who has been involved in a similar situation.

"Any good deer hunter—if he trusts you—will tell you he's seen a deer where there actually was none," says Jack Woolner, of Shrewsbury, Massachusetts, one of the pioneers of hunter safety.

A deer hunter often plies his trade in the gloom of early morning or dusk. These are the peak times of movement for his prey. Experience trains the hunter's eyes to detect movement. Vague shapes and shadings are readily interpreted. Experts refer to it as low-grade information. In the deer woods it's called Early Blur or Visual Closure. As explained in the last chapter, this visual and psychological phenomen can cause an otherwise healthy and normal hunter to see deer where no deer exists.

We know now that in order for Early Blur or Visual Closure to accomplish its potentially deadly work in the deer woods, there must be some clue upon which human perception can build a hypothesis.

It might be a rounded leaf that looks like a buck's ear, a twisted branch that resembles an antler, or maybe a patch of gray or brown that signals the approach of an animal.

"Human vision is a very inexact process," says Woolner, a retired public information officer with the Massachusetts Division of Fisheries & Game. "The best way to explain it is the way a television works.

"Your mind is constantly receiving and decoding electrical signals from three parts of your brain to identify what you're seeing and some of that information is drawn from prior knowledge—not necessarily the exact image you see."

It's been proven, however, that the illusion can be dispelled by providing alternative clues—especially completely incompatible clues.

ORANGE IS UNMISTAKEABLE

It's indisputable that fluorescent orange shatters a dangerous illusion before it can take shape. The color is so startlingly vivid and unnatural that is dispels all "deer clues."

It follows that a hunter wearing fluorescent orange clothing is virtually exempt from being mistaken for game because that color offers no possible clue upon which to base an incorrect hypothesis.

In fact, since the fiery Blaze Orange is unlike anything in nature, it simply has to shout "man-made!"

What is Blaze Orange? Technically, according to the Hunter Education Association, it is a shading "having a dominant wavelength between 595 and 605 nanometers, a luminance factor of not less than 40 percent and an excitation purity of not less than 85 percent."

Got that?

In layman's terms it's a universally recognized, instantly identifiable color that has become a standard in the nation's deer woods.

We're told that fluorescence results when light energy is absorbed by one spectral region and re-emitted by another. In essence, red-orange fluorescent material reflects a normal amount of the spectrum but it also soaks up ultraviolet and blue rays and re-emits them as a red orange to supplement the basic orange.

In short, fluorescent orange is approximately three times as brilliant as a garment of the same color that lacks fluorescent dyes.

Blaze Orange came onto the hunting scene more than 30 years ago. Probably its first exposure through the outdoors press came in 1960 when Field & Stream ran an article entitled "Hunter Orange— Your Shield for Safety".

The article was penned by New England writer Frank Woolner, who documented brother Jack's pioneering research of the fluorescent orange idea.

COLOR AWARENESS RESEARCH

The color wasn't something selected at random. Jack Woolner, then working for the Massachusetts Division of Fisheries and Game, spearheaded a landmark hunter-safety study of colors at Ft. Devens, Mass., in 1959.

Using Army personnel, Woolner's knowledge of hunting conditions and the optical expertise of Dr. Oscar Richards of the American Optical Company and Lt. Jack Panjian, an optometrist at the U.S. Army Hospital at Ft. Devens, the research was conducted in a 2.5-square mile wooded section of the military compound.

"Looking back now we can't imagine how we did it," Jack Woolner said recently. "How were we able to get such cooperation and coordination from the military and vision experts for such a huge undertaking.

"When we made the proposal to the post commander (Maj. General William Verbeck) he thought there might be some military application and gave us the use of the grounds, his full cooperation and a full brigade of his best troops."

Tested under widely varying lighting and atmospheric conditions over three months, 22,346 sightings by 526 men were analyzed. All manner of sophisticated light-interpreting devices were used.

In the tests "standard reds appear near black in shadow areas and disappear under poor light. Yellow, once presented as the best color for hunting by a group in California, is a highly visible color, but appears white (the color of a deer's tail) early and late in the day. In addition a small yellow object, centered on the foveola of the human eye, is not seen. Yellow is also a very common color in nature and it loses most of its limited value at dawn or dusk."

Nearly 9 percent of the male population and 1 percent of the female population have defective color vision that would further confuse reds and greens. Some other color was obviously needed.

A daylight fluorescent orange used by the Army in World War II for tank markers and by the Navy for life boats and flotation vests, was deemed—by a committee of vision experts, state and military officials—most visible under the widest variety of conditions by the widest variety of people.

40 STATES MANDATE ORANGE

According to a 1992 survey by Highland Industries (makers of Ten Mile Cloth and Camo Ten high-visibility fabrics) today 40 states and five Canadian provinces mandate the wearing of fluorescent orange for their deer hunters during the firearms season. The other 10 states and two other provinces are all on record as "strongly recommending" the use of the universal safety color.

In 1961 Massachusetts became the first state to mandate the wearing of fluorescent orange garments by hunters.

The nationwide number of hunting-related accidents, particularly the mistaken-for-game and line-of-fire varieties, have been on a steady decline for more than 20 years, over which span the influence of fluorescent orange has increased dramatically.

It thus requires only minor journalistic license to suggest that the introduction of Blaze Orange to the nation's hunting consciousness is the biggest move toward hunter safety since the invention of manual action-locking devices (safeties) on firearms late in the last century.

It must be noted, however, that despite its history, fluorescent orange is not mandated in 10 states.

It is ironic that New York, the uncontested leader in "grandmotherly" legislation designed to protect people from the exigencies of life, has stood fast against mandatory fluorescent orange over the years.

Lt. Michael O'Hara, head of the state's Department of Environmental Conservation Sportsmen's Education Program, cited a personal survey. He says that survey shows states that mandate the use of fluorescent orange have a higher accidental death rate among hunters than states that do not mandate it.

O'Hara's survey shows that the 40 states that mandate the color have an average death rate of five hunters per 100,000 while the other 10 states average three per 100,000.

The reason?

"In states where orange is not mandatory hunters must use more care before shooting," O'Hara said. "Knowing that there might be someone in the woods not wearing orange, they are more likely to follow a basic safety rule—fully identify the target before pulling the trigger."

ORANGE NOT THE ANSWER?

His survey of states mandating orange showed a compliance rate of 70 to 90 percent. He estimates that 80 percent of New York's 700,000 hunters already wear some fluorescent orange.

While attending a meeting of the New York Conservation Fund Advisory Council in 1992 he noted: "The required use of Blaze Orange conveys the wrong message, that each person's responsibility is to not become a victim. The right message is that it is each person's responsibility to be certain of the target before shooting."

Other states, while recommending the use of fluorescent orange, have stopped short of mandating it due to an "old boys' network" among the decision makers, according to Jack Woolner.

The general feeling among this group is that the gaudy color is a signal that alerts and alarms deer.

These people offer no explanation of how a state like Pennsylvania, which requires each of its 1.2 million deer hunters to wear 250 square inches of fluorescent orange afield, can harvest up to 350,000 whitetails annually.

The Pennsylvania Game Commission points out that of the 30 highest annual buck harvests on record, 29 of them have come in the last 29 years—the last 13 with all hunters wearing Blaze Orange.

Having on many occasions shot advancing deer, oblivious to my presence despite my very visible orange vest, I suggest that if deer do see the color they are not alarmed by it. Not a wit.

Movement, however, is a different story.

There has been research that shows that deer do have the visual capacity of seeing colors in the fluorescent orange spectrum. There's no dispute that the color's brightness and intensity does draw attention to any movement the hunter might make—which surely alarms deer.

The personal theory is to limit the orange display to the torso, if your hunting venue (ie: local regulations) allows it. Display on extremities, such as gloves, hats, sleeves, pant legs, etc., is more likely to betray movement.

"The feeling has long been that the sight of Hunter Orange doesn't trigger an automatic fear response in deer," said Jack Woolner. "When you think about it, throughout history and for 11 months every year a deer's natural predators are dark."

Fellow fluorescent orange pioneer Dr. Richards, now resident lecturer at Pacific University of Optometry, has another theory.

Dr. Richards once told Frank Woolner, "some emphasis that the likely greater brightness may be an attractant to deer should be given equal time...."

Now there's a theory that needs exploring.

BLAZE ORANGE REGULATIONS

State	Square inches required
ALABAMA	144, all sides (no camo orange)
ARKANSAS	400 above waist
COLORADO	500 above waist (no camo orange)
CONNECTICUT	400 above waist
DELAWARE	400, head, chest and back
FLORIDA	500 above waist
GEORGIA	500 above waist
HAWAII	144 above waist
ILLINOIS	400, cap and above waist (no camo orange)
INDIANA	Some visible (no camo orange)
IOWA	Some visible (no camo orange)
KANSAS	Some, hat, front & back
KENTUCKY	Some, head, chest, back (no camo orange)
LOUISIANA	400, Head, chest, back
MAINE	Some, hat and torso (no camo orange)
MARYLAND	Some, cap and vest
MASSACHUSETTS	500 above waist
MICHIGAN	Some visible all sides
MINNESOTA	Some above waist
MISSISSIPPI	500 visible all sides (no camo orange)
MISSOURI	Some visible all sides (no camo orange)
MONTANA	400 above waist
NEBRASKA	400, head, back, chest
NEW JERSEY	200 visible all sides
NORTH CAROLINA	Some visible all sides
NORTH DAKOTA	400 above waist (no camo orange)
OHIO	Some, hat, vest or coat
OKLAHOMA	500 above waist (400 must be solid)
PENNSYLVANIA	250, head, chest and back
RHODE ISLAND	200 above waist (no camo orange)
SOUTH CAROLINA	Some, hat, coat or vest (no camo orange)
SOUTH DAKOTA	Some above waist
TENNESSEE	500, hat and above waist
TEXAS	144, hat and torso
VIRGINIA	100 visible all sides (no camo orange)
UTAH	400 above waist

BLAZE ORANGE REGULATIONS, Cont'd

State	Square inches required
WASHINGTON	400 above waist
WEST VIRGINIA	400 visible all sides
WISCONSIN	Some, 50 % above waist
WYOMING	Some visible

CANADIAN PROVINCES

MANITOBA	400 head, chest, back
NEW BRUNSWICK	400 chest, back (No camo orange)
NOVA SCOTIA	Some, hat, vest, coat
QUEBEC	400 visible all angles
SASKATCHEWAN	Complete outer suit (No camo orange)

NOTE: Alaska, Arizona, California, Idaho, Nevada, New Hampshire, New Mexico, New York, Oregon, Vermont, Newfoundland, Northwest Territories, Ontario and Prince Edward Island do not mandate the wearing of fluorescent orange but strongly recommend its use during firearms seasons.

Only Alberta and British Columbia have no requirements and make no recommendations.

(Information provided by Highland Industries, 1994)

"Menet sub iove frigido Venator Tenerae coniugis immemor" (The hunter goes his way 'neath frigid skies unmindful of his tender spouse) —Homer

PART VII:

HOW-TO

Chapter 29
Keeping Score in the Outdoors

"Nice rack. What's it score?"

That statement pretty much sums up the prevalent sentiment among whitetail hunters today.

Those booking guided hunts for whitetails in Canadian Maritimes, or the western prairies of the U.S. and Canada are often looking for "160 bucks" or that ultra-elusive "book buck"—meaning one with a rack that measures large enough to qualify for the famed Boone & Crockett record book of big game trophies.

"The Book" wasn't always the Bible that it represents today. Though Boone and Crockett backed the formation of the National Collection of Heads and Horns during Teddy Roosevelt's day, for scientific purposes, its original charter in 1887 stipulated that it was a broad-based conservation organization, active in calling for the setting aside of forest preserves, demanding limited hunting seasons, promulgating the rules of fair chase, etc.

The Roosevelt Luckey buck from New York was once the Boone & Crockett world record in both typical and non-typical scoring.

Critics charge that the Boone & Crockett system is not a fair evaluation because it penalizes some racks more than others.

The Club didn't actually start keeping record books until 1932. Because many hunters felt the B&C system was unfair to racks that didn't have extreme symmetry and spread, other systems were formed. The only one that gained even a modicum of acceptance was the 1977 introduction of the Safari Club International system, which is much less rigorous in its scoring criteria and thus allows more animals to qualify.

SHOOTING FOR THE 'BOOK'

But entry in the Boone & Crockett book has become the Holy Grail of trophy hunters and its scoring system, regardless of drawbacks and controversy, is the universal yardstick for comparison of whitetails. The system is the basis for virtually all state and re-

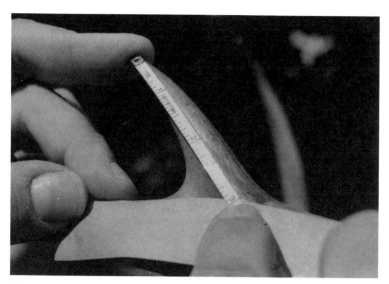

Tine measurements are one of several dimensions used in Boone & Crockett scoring.

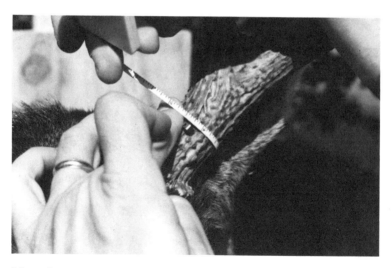

Mass is measured by taking beam circumfrence measurements in a variety of spots.

New York State Big Buck Club
90 Maxwell Road • Caledonia, New York 14423

NONTYPICAL WHITE-TAILED DEER

E. Abnormal Points	
Left	Right
Totals	
To Line E	

FINAL SCORE

MINIMUM SCORE:
GUN 165
ARCHERY 145

DEER TAKEN WITH:
☐ GUN
☐ MUZZLELOADER
☐ ARCHERY

See Other Side for Instructions		Supplementary Data		Column 1	Column 2	Column 3	Column 4
		L.	R.	Spread Credit	Left Antler	Right Antler	Difference
A. Number of Points on Each Antler							
B. Tip to Tip Spread							
C. Greatest Spread							
D. Inside Spread of Main Beams		Spread credit may equal but not exceed length of longer beam					
If Inside Spread exceeds longer beam length, enter difference							
E. Total of Length of All Abnormal Points							
F. Length of Main Beam							
G-1. Length of First Point, if present							
G-2. Length of Second Point							
G-3. Length of Third Point							
G-4. Length of Fourth Point, if present							
G-5. Length of Fifth Point, if present							
G-6 Length of Sixth Point, if present							
G-7. Length of Seventh Point, if present							
H-1. Circumference at Smallest Place Between Burr and G-1							
H-2. Circumference at Smallest Place Between G-1 and G-2							
H-3. Circumference at Smallest Place Between G-2 and G-3							
H-4. Circumference at Smallest Place Between G-3 and G-4							
TOTALS							

ADD	Column 1		Kill Location: Town	County
	Column 2		Date killed	Name
	Column 3		Present owner	
Total			Address	City State Zip
SUBTRACT Column 4			Date measured	Owner's Phone #
Result			Remarks: (Mention any abnormalities)	
Add Line E Total				
FINAL SCORE				

11

Many organizations use the Boone & Crockett scoring system.

gional record-keeping organizations as well as the international Pope & Young Society for bowhunting.

"I really didn't realize how big a buck has to be to make the book until we measured mine," said Phil Ryan of Trumansburg, NY. Ryan, a 23-year-old bricklayer, was hunting in eastern Saskatchewan in 1993 when he shot a 16-point buck that not only qualified for the Boone & Crockett record book but also made the top five in the National Muzzleloaders Association's Long Rifle Society record books. "He was by far the biggest buck anybody in camp had ever seen and he just made it by a few inches."

In fact, it's been estimated that only one buck in a million wears headgear large enough to qualify for the Boone & Crockett book. For comparison, most hunters would consider a buck in the 120 range to be a trophy. A 140 buck is a spectacular prize for 99 percent of today's hunters and a "150" is the buck of a lifetime for all but a handful of full-time trophy hunters.

As a licensed guide in Idaho I advise my hunters that a rack that extends wider than the ears (at least 18 inches outside spread) and stands clearly above the extended ears is at least a 130 buck.

Ryan's Saskatchewan buck, killed with a .54-caliber muzzleloader that Ryan and his father built themselves, gross-scored 205 7/8ths and was scored 176 4/8ths as a typical and 200 1/8 as a non-typical. The B&C book minimum for typicals is 170 and for non-typicals 195. Measurements may be recorded only after a 60-day drying period, during which the rack loses much of its moisture and thus shrinks. A rack that is borderline as a qualifier will lose as much as 2-3 inches in that 60-day period.

Those are impressive figures to throw around, but how many people actually know what they mean? And what's a typical or a non-typical? It turns out that a lot more people think they know than actually do.

The Boone & Crockett system records, in 1/8ths of an inch, the size of a rack, measuring beam length, inside spread, the length of up to seven tines on either beam and beam circumferences from up to four locations on each beam.

If a rack is scored as a "typical" all the measurements are added and any abnormal points and differences in corresponding measurements between sides is deducted to get the final score.

Confusing?

SCORING A RACK

Okay, let's assume you're scoring a 10-point (eastern count) rack as a typical. A typical 10-point will have matched brow tines (G-1 in scoring parlance), matched long second tines at or near the top of the curve of the rack (G-2), matched third tines (G-3) and matched fourth tines (G-4). The fifth point on either beam is the point of the beam and is not measured. If you view a symmetrical rack from the side the near side will often obscure the far side. Anything that doesn't match up—extra tines on one side or abnormal growths—are subtracted from the gross score, as are the differences between corresponding tines and circumference measurements.

"Non-typicals are scored the same way," said certified scorer Merritt Compton of New York. "In the rack you're describing you'd score the basic frame as a 10-point and make the deductions for symmetry, just as you would for a typical. The only difference is that where you would subtract the "E" measurement (abnormal growth) to get a typical score, you would add that measurement to get the non-typical score."

Today racks may be measured as typicals and non-typicals but are usually entered in the books in whatever category they rank highest. But in the early days of scoring, when entries were scarce, the same rack could dominate both categories.

For instance, the New York State record typical, a 14-pointer killed in 1939 that measured 198 2/8ths, for some time was the Boone & Crockett No. 1 in both the typical and non-typical (221 6/8ths). The farmer who killed the buck, Roosevelt Luckey of Hume, NY, had the buck scored in the 1940s. Several other racks taken before Luckey's were measured in subsequent years and moved his down in the books.

Still find the scoring system confusing? Let's take a look at a scoresheet and go through the measuring system.

The scoresheet first requests three measurements that aren't included in the scoring—just identifying data: the number of points on each antler, the tip-to-tip spread, and the greatest spread.

To be counted as point under the B&C system, a projection must be at least one inch long and its length must exceed the width of its base. All points are measured from the tip of the point to the nearest edge of the beam. The beam tip is counted as point but not measured as a point.

The tip-to-tip spread is self-explanatory while the greatest spread is a measurement taken at right angles to the center line of the skull at the rack's widest part, whether across the main beams or points.

The inside spread, line D on the scoring sheet, is the first measurement that counts in the scoring. If it is longer than the length of the longer of the two beams, the measurement is subtracted rather than added to the score.

Line E is a measurement of all abnormal points—those non-typical in shape or location like drop tines, etc. This measurement is subtracted from a typical score and added to a non-typical score.

Line F is the main beams, measured from the lowest outside edge of the burr over the outer curve to the most distant point of what is or appears to be the main beam. The point of beginning is that point on the burr where the center line along the outer curve intersects the burr. Differences in length are subtracted from the score.

The "G" measurements are those of the normal individual points, up to seven per beam. The measurement is taken from the nearest edge of the main beam (often outlined by a piece of tape) over the outer curve of the tine to the tip. Differences in the lengths of corresponding points is subtracted from the score.

The "H" measurements are four beam circumferences, starting with the smallest cirumference between the burr and the brow tine (H-1), then the smallest circumference figure between the brow tine and the G-2 point (H-2). The H-3 measurement is the smallest spot between G-2 and G-3 and H-4 is a similar measurement between G-3 and G-4. If there is no G-4 tine (six-point rack), the H-4 measurement is taken at a position halfway between the G-3 tine and the beam tip.

As with al l the "G" or tine measurements, differences between corresponding "H" measurements are subtracted from the total in both typical and non-typical scoring.

"A lot of guys scoring for themselves will measure all the points (instead of stopping at seven per beam) and all the circumfrences (instead of the first four)," Compton said. "And some won't subtract the differences when they're quoting a non-typical score. You can get some pretty impressive scores that way, but it's not accurate under the system."

The system of scoring a typical rack obviously rewards symmetry—some people say to an extreme, penalizing spectacularly massive racks of typical configuration because they don't match up precisely side-to-side.

UNFAIR COMPARISON?

The new world record typical (pending review) is a long-tined Saskatchewan buck killed November 1993 by local farmer Milo Hanson. The 12-point rack net scored 213 1/8ths as a typical, fully eight inches larger than the previous record buck, a 206 1/8th 10-point killed in 1914 by the late James Jordan of Danbury, Wisconsin. Many normal-framed racks larger than Jordan's—better racks in some eyes—had been scored over the intervening 80 years but none boasted the phenomenal symmetry.

It has been argued that the Hanson and Jordan bucks were both freaks—"non-typical" in a common sense approach in that they were so incredibly symmetrical. The Hanson buck, for instance, grossed 221 inches—about the same as the Luckey buck in New York state—with about 4.5 inches deducted for side-to-side differences and another 2.5 inches of abnormal growth, constituted by two points growing off tines. The Luckey buck, by comparison, dropped 6 1/8th in side-to-side differences and 8 5/8ths in abnormal growth.

"In Boone & Crockett it's not what the deer has on its head, it's how much is there after you imagine so much is missing," said Russell Thornberry, whitetail author, magazine editor and former guide and outfitter. "That's BC's problem. I like every little thing they grow."

Another case against the fairness of the B&C system involved a massive buck taken in Illinois in 1993 by Brian Damery of Macon County, Ill.

The buck is the highest grossing score for a typical (before deductions for symmetry) category buck ever taken, 231 1/8ths inches. By comparison the Hanson buck grossed 221 1-8ths. The Damery buck had an inside spread of 28 6/8ths inches, the widest among the top 10 typicals in the Boone & Crockett book. And the main beam lengths of 32 2/8ths and 31 5/8ths are the longest in the history of the venerable scoring system.

Damery's net score of 200 2/8ths (all scoring is done in 8ths, not rounded) will put it in the top 10 all-time in the typical category despite the fact that it dwarfs all other typical category bucks ever taken.

Another knock on the Boone & Crockett system is the gray areas in the scoring criteria that leave certain judgements up to the scorer—decisions that other scorers may not see the same way. For instance, three years ago a huge 20-point Alberta buck made a splash as a potential world record typical when measured at 209 by a local scorer. But a subsequent measuring session by other certified scorers dropped the score considerably.

"The Koberstein rack could have been scored anywhere from 187 to 209 typical, given interpretation by the individual scorer," said a B&C representative in Alberta.

Perhaps the biggest controversy comes in the scoring of large non-typicals, since scorer interpretation can play a huge part in what constitutes a beam, abnormal or deductible growth, etc.

The current Boone & Crockett world record non-typical scores 333 7/8ths. The rack was from a buck found dead along a Missouri highway in 1982. Another spectacular non-typical was found dead early in this century along railroad trucks in Kent, Ohio, and wasn't measured until the mid-1980s after it was "discovered" hanging in a barroom by a trophy-scorer. The Kent buck, now known as the "Hole In the Horn" buck due to a .22-caliber bullet horn in one beam, was scored several times by a variety of scorers—most of whom scored it higher than the Missouri record rack. But the final scoring showed it to be about four inches shy of the Missouri rack, despite some obvious advantages when the two racks are viewed together.

Despite its obvious drawbacks and controversies, and ignoring the ethical questions of keeping score in the outdoors at all, the Boone & Crockett system is the one today's trophy hunter uses to determine success.

"Most of us know that taxidermists' work is not equal. A $100 deerhead may sound like a real bargain but may look like one of those Star Trek villians."

Chapter 30
Selecting a Good Deer Taxidermist

Invariably the first question asked a taxidermist during hunting season is "What do you get for a deer head?"

Granted, price is a consideration. That's only natural. But you wouldn't make a decision on buying a new rifle or shotgun without first seeing and holding it. You wouldn't buy a used pickup based on a telephone description—not until you'd seen and driven it.

So why on earth would anyone trust their hunting trophies to a taxidermist based solely on a telephone price check? Taxidermy work is, after all, a luxury. That shoulder mount isn't a matter of survival, it's a conversation piece; decoration; a trophy.

Yet many taxidermy purchase decisions are made based on a price quoted over the telephone. When I was a running a full-time taxidermy studio I allowed no price quoting over the telephone. Go see a taxidermist's work, I suggested. If it's good enough, then talk about price. If the quality isn't there, no price is good. Then I asked when they wanted to visit the studio.

It's been said that the attitude cost me business. I prefer to see it as weeding out "bargain seekers", not the folks who could afford and appreciate quality work. Granted, the final ticket is a factor in choosing a taxidermist, but it may well be the least important.

Taxidermist Bill Yox of Brockport, New York was named the National Taxidermist Association's Taxidermist of the Year in 1991.

Today's whitetail taxidermy verges on an art form.

A comparison of today's professional sculpted foam forms (Buck-eye Manikins) and an 80-year-old form that included parts of the deer's skull and jaws.

Most of us know that taxidermists' work is not equal. A $100 deerhead may sound like a real bargain but may look like one of those Star Trek villians.

The good news is that quality taxidermy is more widely available than ever. Given the advanced state of today's whitetail taxidermy forms, techniques and instruction, there is no reason to accept a less than life-like mount. All you have to know is what to look for in a taxidermist.

TAXIDERMY IS PROGRESSING

It's safe to say that the craft progressed more in the last 25 years than it did in the previous 200, and that rate of progress doesn't show any signs of slowing.

In fact, whitetail mounts that earned me blue ribbons in state competition in the mid-1980s probably wouldn't even rate an honorable mention award today.

Actually until a couple of decades ago taxidermy was pretty much a black art—a craft conducted alone, in dank, inhospitable

Today's taxidermists are able to put expression into mounts that was never possible before.

The lifelike detail around the nose and mouth is usually used for competition mounts but just shows the level to which deer taxidermy has risen.

This live deer demonstrates that the antlers come off the skull at roughly the same angle as the slope of nose.

environs. Practitioners didn't share ideas, techniques or even general information. The craft was passed on only to apprentices and eldest sons.

But in the early 1970s the National Taxidermist Association was formed as were state and regional groups. Seminars were held; ideas shared. Schools opened; instructional videos became available. The heightened awareness and expanded horizons meant a bigger market, more competition and quantum leaps forward in terms of form design, eyes, materials, techniques and equipment.

"Whitetail taxidermy today has risen to an art form," said Bill Yox of Brockport, NY, former NTA Taxidermist of the Year. "There are so many more things that can be done with a mount today. But not every taxidermist has the knowledge or skill to take advantage of the advances."

Yox first suggests doing your "scouting" for a taxidermist before the hunting season. Shops are apt to be very busy and perhaps cluttered after opening day and the taxidermist may not have time to devote to your questions, etc.

Knowing what to look for in a quality mount is the key, and the questions to ask should provide a solid foundation for your decision.

"Other than looking for the real obvious things—are the eyes focused in the same direction, are they set right, do the ears look right—there's some other things I tell prospective customers to look for in a good mount," said Yox, who won the 1992 Bruhac Award for best whitetail mount in national competition.

"Are the seams showing; are too much of the lips showing; does the buck look like it's smiling."

Yox also says to see if all the features fit together—if the eyes are in a relaxed pose, how about the ears? If white shows at the rear of one eye it should show at the front of the other.

Joe Millham of Mountain Rest Taxidermy in Gardiner, NY, has won ribbons in both world and national competition.

"I tell people to look from antlers down when they're judging a taxidermist's work," said Millham, who mounts as many at 250 deer heads each year. "The average person gets so tied up in antler size that they never really look at the mount."

That has long been a problem in deer taxidermy. Most people want the head mounted because of the antler size—the mount itself is secondary. That's why you see so many bug-eyed, smirking whitetail mounts.

"I tell people to look for symmetry," Millham said. "Is the brisket centered or off to one side. Are both the eyes level? How about the ears?"

FINDING LOCAL TAXIDERMISTS

Okay, we've established that the first step is going to see the taxidermist's work. But how do you find a taxidermist?

The Yellow Pages of your telephone directory is a sensible place to start, although many excellent taxidermists—particularly those that are hobbyists—don't advertise.

Most good taxidermists are well known to local sporting goods stores and sportsmen's clubs—but don't take a clerk's or colleague's opinion about a taxidermist's talent. A studio that does a lot of work isn't necessarily a good one—just established or well-located.

You can also check with the National Taxidermist Association (108 Branch Dr., Slidell, LA 70461. Tel: 504-641-4NTA) or the International Guild of Taxidermy (PO Box 95, South Beloit, WI 61080-0095. Tel: 608-884-8177) for information on your state chapter. From there you should be able to get a listing of members in your area.

Not all good taxidermists are members of organizations, but it is a good place to start your search. Besides, membership in these organizations exposes a taxidermist to all of the latest techniques, products and ideas—not to mention competitions.

Granted, a head done for competition gets a lot more attention and detail than a customer's mount, but a taxidermist who has won awards can generally be counted on to do good commercial work. The differences between his (or her) competition and commercial work are often so subtle that they would probably not be readily detectable to the average consumer anyway.

And experience isn't necessarily the mark of a good taxidermist, either. I know of men who've been at it 50 years and still set eyes or antlers incorrectly. I've also seen young people with experience measured in months win blue ribbons in state competition with heads they mounted while at taxidermy school.

But again, don't trust word-of-mouth. Go to the taxidermists' shop and take a close look at the work.

WHAT DO YOU LOOK FOR?

So when you get there, what do you look for?

The most often abused feature of any whitetail mount is the eyes. They're called the soul of the mount—the thing you notice first (after the antlers). When viewed from the front, are they both focused on you? Are the thin blue pupils both level? Does the deer look bug-eyed?

Today's textbook mounting procedures call for the eyes to be set at 45-degree angles to the center of the nose and tilted in 9 degrees top-to-bottom. But it doesn't take an angle gauge to tell if the taxidermist knows what he or she is doing when setting eyes. Poorly set eyes are immediately noticeable—they just don't look right.

Next check the ears. The bottoms of the earbutts on a whitetail deer should be no lower than the bottom of the eye. It's very easy, when stretching the hide onto the form, to mount the ears too low—and very noticeable once you know what to look for. The ears should be thin with the white hair entirely inside.

The black of the lips should show only slightly—about the width of the nose black—unless the mount has an open mouth. On a competition mount the inside of the nostrils is flesh-colored or pink but most customers don't request that degree of realism.

Nevertheless, nose hair should be entirely inside the nostrils and not stretched outside. And with today's mounts it isn't necessary to fill the nostrils with wax—they should have depth.

The angle of the antlers is often abused by poorly trained taxidermists. Viewed from the side, the antlers should come off a whitetail's head at roughly the same angle as the slope of the nose.

As Millham said, the brisket line should be centered and the flaired hair equal on either side. You'll sometimes see the brisket flair mounted too high on the neck if the hide was stretched too much.

HOW WAS HIDE PREPARED?

If you like the look of the work, ask the taxidermist if he or she (two of the best whitetail taxidermists in the country are women) uses tanned hides. A professionally tanned hide is expensive but durable and there are some excellent shop tanning processes available.

Yox, for example, uses commercial tanners while Millham's big-volume business requires shop tanning.

Many taxidermists use dry preservative to cure hides for mounts, particularly in the south. Dry preservative is a quick and inexpensive means of preserving the skin, but can lead to cracks and distorted features when the mount dries—particularly if the hide is not properly prepared or if the mount is displayed in an area where humidity flucuates widely.

"I think dry preservative has a place in taxidermy," Millham said. "But not for deer heads. It's just too hard to tell how well the head will hold up in later years."

Taxidermist Stan Gould of Sardinia, Ohio, agrees: "You can tell a dry preservative head from across the room. It just gets ratty looking real quick."

On the other hand many award-winning taxidermists use dry preservative wirh excellent results. Some say that the talent or experience of the practitioner makes the difference, not the method of preserving the hide.

Dry preservative is a very controversial subject in the taxidermy field. Successful users often have years of experience in handling and thinning hides and live in a climate with plenty of constant humidity may be the reason.

But one very experienced and talented Pennsylvania taxidermist switched to dry preservative for two years and saw more than 2/3rds of his deer heads returned due to splitting hides. He admits that he probably thinned the hides too much—but he doesn't use dry preservative any more.

At the same time, Dan Chase of Louisiana, a taxidermist for more than 30 years and the owner of a major taxidermy supply company, points out that orders for his dry preservative have skyrocketed in the last decade.

"I don't know what other companies put in their dry preservative but we've never had any problems . . . I think you'll find a lot more problems with tanned hides."

But dry preservative simply isn't for everyone.

"For a while there it seemed like everyone out here tried (dry preservative). It was fast and easy," said Bob Esposito of Blooming-ton, Ill.—past president of the Illinois Taxidermist Association—who was addressing a conference in Peoria, Ill.

"But too many problems cropped up and hardly anyone here uses it anymore. It just isn't the answer in this area."

One look at a taxidermist's older mounts will tell you if his or her preserving process is adequate.

You should now ask about turn-around time, if that's important to you. Keep in mind that a busy shop will take longer.

Some shops are so busy or specialized that they might wholesale their deer mounts to other taxidermists. It may sound strange, but be sure to ask any studio if they do their own heads or sub-contract the work.

Only when you're satisfied with quality, methods and time frame should the price enter into your decision.

As I said earlier, the price can be misleading. The most expensive taxidermist isn't necessarily the best, nor the least expensive the worst.

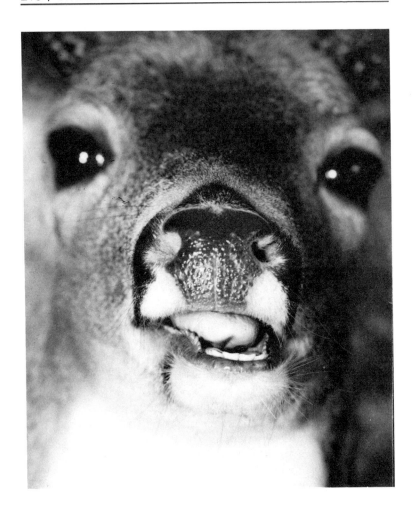

Never choose a taxidermist without seeing his or her work first.

What a taxidermist charges for a mount often depends on many factors other than quality: Is it a full-time shop or is taxidermy a hobby or avocation for the practitioner? Is the pricing based on business sense or on what his competition charges? Is the price designed to bring in customers or to attract more select traffic?

For example, two national award winning taxidermists operated in my area but charged less than other, less talented craftsmen. Both worked at a major corporation and taxidermy was just a hobby. Neither man advertised but both were flooded with work.

You can figure that about 12–14 hours of labor and anywhere from $30 to $85 in materials and expenses go into a whitetail shoulder mount—not to mention talent and business overhead. I've seen prices from $75 to $650. I read a couple of years ago that the national average for a shoulder mount is a little over $200.

Chances are if you know what to look for in a taxidermist—and you find it—the price will be right.

"There are two spiritual dangers in not living on a farm. One is the danger of supposing that breakfast comes from a grocery, and the other that heat comes from a furnace." —Aldo Leopold

PART VIII:

THE BOUNTY

Chapter 31
Venison from Field to Table

We were still newlyweds, living in a basement apartment, when venison first entered our marriage.

Coming as we did from families of hunters, we both had eaten deer meat prepared by our mothers. I loved it. Debbie tolerated it.

But realizing how much hunting meant to her new spouse and how far the meat went toward easing the burden of the grocery budget, Debbie was eager to apply her culinary talents to that first venison meal.

Those talents, however, were very limited at that point in her life. Her mother's instructions usually augmented said talents, but mom wasn't home.

Undaunted, Debbie tackled the situation in true pioneer fashion—she took her husband's advice: brown some onions and fry the two steaks with them 90 seconds on each side to retain the meat's moisture.

Debbie literally beamed as she served the succulence on TV trays (it was a small apartment). She was estatic when her husband savored his first bite and nodded approval.

She was still beaming when she took her first bite. But after two chews her smile waned. It was gone after the third chew. Her face took on an ashen pallor and she bolted for the bathroom. After her digestive tract reversed its normal function, she steadied herself against the nearest wall and offered some loud, strong suggestions on what should be done with this and future deer meat.

It was her first, and last, experience with vension "take-it-or-leave-it" style. Some of us like the taste, others don't. Fortunately for our marriage the cooler head prevailed that day—I ate both steaks and she headed for my previously ignored library of deer books to seek a remedy.

Today she makes a breaded venison tenderloin that would make

the ghost of Escoffer writhe with envy. Rolled neck roasts, marinated steaks and butterfly chops, venison parmesan, venison meatballs, venison piccatta, venison diane and an assortment of ground venison casseroles and dishes are staples in our household and are eagerly anticipated by both of us. She has, in fact, co-authored the book "VENISON: A Users Manual for Deer Hunters" with me and that book shares this chapter.

We gain no pleasure in trying to "trick" an avowed anti-venison person into eating a well-prepared (some call it disguised) piece of deer meat. Heck no. If they don't want it, let's not waste it; it's their loss. We haven't bought beef in more than 10 years, venison and elk meat filling our red meat budget.

THAT VENISON TASTE

Depending as heavily on venison as we do means that we use a variety of means to neutralize the various factors that might give venison a "gamey" taste. I'm not talking about the distinctive flavor imparted by what the animal ate. Venison from a Pennsylvania deer that lived in a laurel patch will differ slightly in taste from that of an Alabama deer that dined regularly on honeysuckle or an Oklahoma whitetail from sage country or an alfalfa and corn-fed deer from farm country.

No, the taste we seek to neutralize comes from the meat's condition, how long it was aged, how it was dressed and its state at the time it was killed.

Knowing and dealing with these conditions can mean the difference between delightful table fare and something resembling Fido's bedding.

For instance, if the meat was aged too long or improperly—we're not talking spoiled but rather strong-smelling—you can bet it's going to have that famed "gamey" taste. If the animal was very stressed before death, either by a poorly placed shot or a hard run, the meat is apt to be dark and sticky. It's depleted, not acidic like the muscles of a relaxed animal, and thus more prone to spoilage.

Many venison experts advise coating the meat of a stressed animal in vinegar; add the missing acidity. Others say marinate it in olive oil or Italian dressing.

You may also find that the meat of an older buck, particularly one that has been rutting, will be tougher and will have a stronger taste. We treat this meat the same way we do that of a stressed deer. Soak the meat in milk for 4-6 hours in the refrigerator. This can be done after the meat is thawed or while it's thawing.

The meat of a stressed deer, by the way, should not be aged. Get the hide off, cut it up and freeze it as soon as possible. Because of the lack of acidity it provides an excellent medium for bacterial growth; hence the strong smell and/or propensity to spoil quickly.

All blood-shot portions should be removed entirely and the surrounding meat soaked in salt water in the refrigerator for a couple of hours to draw out the blood in the tissue.

Proper butchering and preparation can make delectable table fare of any cut of meat from any deer, regardless of shot placement, the animal's age or sex, how far it ran, or curing time. If you can't cut across the grain of the meat, one of the great equalizers is to slice the cut very thin—a half inch isn't too thin—and pound it with a tenderizing mallet or butcher knife. Break down the fibers and you'll be able to cut it with a fork without using any additives.

WHY HANG CARCASS?

Some meat experts claim that since deer meat does not have fat marbled through it like beef, there is no advantage to hanging the carcass. This group suggests getting the hide off the animal immediately to release body heat as quickly as possible, then cutting, wrapping and freezing the meat the same day. This meat can be aged somewhat by defrosting it in a refrigerator for a couple of days.

Others suggest that you age the meat to break down muscle fiber and thus tenderize the meat before butchering. The latter philosophy is the most widely practiced.

There is, by the way, a right way to age a carcass. Ideally the skinned carcass should be hung, neck down, in controlled temperatures of 34-36 degrees in 40 to 50 percent humidity for several days. That's ideal for tenderizing the meat and keeping moisture in it. But how many of us have those controlled conditions in our garage, shed or front yard maple tree?

It's obviously better to leave it to a professional who has a meat cooler. I shy away from those processors who cut meat with a bandsaw—spreading the bone marrow and sinew. Have the meat boned, take out the back loin and cut it into butterfly chops rather than having it sawed pork shop style. Then have it double-wrapped, air tight, for freezer storage.

VENISON TIPS:

Here are some things to keep in mind when dealing with venison:

* Marinating venison is a good means of changing or disguising its taste and sometimes of tenderizing the meat. But marinating does rob the meat of some of its nutrients.
* High heat can quickly dry out and toughen a cut of venison. Cook slowly and sparingly. Wild game meat has no fat. Use fat or oil to provide moisture while cooking.
* Although venison is touted as a health food, some cuts actually have more cholestrol than beef.
* Ground venison is usually prepared with beef suet or pork fat mixed in to provide moisture and fat.
* Any organs considered for table fare—heart, liver, kidneys—

should be soaked in salt water for a couple of hours to draw out the blood. Organ meat is best eaten the same day the animal is killed. It can be frozen but loses some of its taste.

* Properly wrapped (double-wrapped in freezer paper, air tight) can be stored in a freezer for more than a year without a loss of flavor or texture.

* Thawed venison in a transparent wrap should only be stored in refrigerator for up to two days. Meat wrapped in brown paper may be refrigerated three to five days but should be unwrapped, placed on a platter or tray and loosely covered.

Chapter 32
Whaddya Think He Weighs?

A cynic might have viewed it as less than a definitive study. Granted, there was no isolated culture or sophisticated monitoring devices and no federal grant was obtained to fund the research.

The control area, in fact, was the dimly lit parking lot of a small but busy grocery-butcher shop in a small Northeastern city. And the total research budget was the cost of a cold six-pack.

It was a chilled November night late in the last decade and my scholarly quest was to determine how accurately hunters could guess the weight of a white-tailed deer. Being a journalist, I was seeking the ultimate truth—so long as it could be ascertained within the parameters established by the time it would take my research analyst to put away the half-dozen cold ones.

Realizing the importance of keeping a sharp mind during research, and also realizing the slimness of the chance of my getting any of the beer, I opted for coffee.

The shop was a long-standing favorite for deer butchering and there was a steady stream of hunters and deer carcasses coming and going. An ideal test area if ever I've seen one.

The control subject was a large doe that earlier that day donated her body to research, with my help. The shop owner was a loud-mouthed sort who stood with me, dutifully fortifying himself against the cold with the contents of my six-pack while soliciting opinions on the approximate weight of our departed pal.

"I've been cutting meat for almost 30 years and I can tell you within five pounds exactly what she weighs," he blustered between quaffs.

"Hey you. Whaddya think she'll weigh?"

Each observer's guess was met with a deprecating laugh from the butcher-expert and dutifully recorded by me. The traffic was there and I'd hoped to solicit 100 opinions. But the butcher finished

the six-pack—and thus the questioning—at 62, so science will have to accept our findings on that basis.

Everyone questioned agreed that she was a monster doe for our neck of the woods. The resultant 82 guesses ranged from 175 pounds to 500 pounds, the latter proffered by a disheveled young lad who wandered out of a nearby alley, apparently bemused by some mind-bending chemical.

The last can emptied, our expert crushed it in his fist, belched and slowly shook his head in disgust over the recorded guesses.

"You're all full of crap. She's the biggest we've had so far this season and she'll only go about 140," said the butcher as two of his lackeys hoisted the guest of honor to his scales. "They're never as big as people think."

He didn't even wait for the official announcement, walking instead to his shop while the scale's needle still wavered.

The shop door closed behind him just as the needle steadied at 142 pounds.

ACTUAL SIZE IS DECEIVING

Most hunters can tell you the number of antler points and the weight of every buck they see in the field. And most would be astonished—and would probably back up that disbelief with belligerence—to learn that a good-sized buck would barely reach the average man's belt buckle.

Hunters' weight estimates on deer, inflated as they invariably are by adrenaline and sheer ignorance, are worse than fishermen's claims. One cannot readily reach into a tackle box to find a scale capable of settling an argument on the size of a 6-point buck.

The rule of thumb for determining live weight is to add one-third to the hog-dressed weight—but that's of no use without a suitable set of scales.

Penn State University and the Pennsylvania Game Commission devised a table based on heart girth measurements (place tape around chest just behind forelegs) that determines the approximate weight of the deer live, field dressed and hog-dressed plus the weight of the hide, the blood, the bone and the amount of edible meat.

The average buck taken in New York and Pennsylvania, for instance, is 1.5 years old and field dresses at around 120 pounds, according to wildlife biologists from those states. The heart girth is in the neighborhood of 36 inches.

There are more than 30 subspecies of whitetails, however, and sizes can vary significantly with geology.

MEASURING SYSTEM

Minnesota hunter-writer Jeff Murray has handicapped the measuring procedure to adapt it to various regions of the country. In his book, "For Big Bucks Only" (North American Hunting Club, 1989), Murray says the field dressed weight for a deep south buck, including Texas, is 5.6 X the heart girth, minus 94.

Field-dressed weight of the big deer of the upper midwest can be ascertained, according to Murray, by multiplying the heart girth by 7.7 and subtracting 178. Virtually anywhere else it's a matter of multiplying the girth measurement by 6.5 and subtracting 120.

The farther from the equator a subspecies lives, the larger the body will tend to be, according to a loose interpretation of a biological law known as Bergman's Rule.

The average adult buck (they reach full skeletal size at 4.5 to 5.5 years) in the northern regions of this continent, for instance, approaches 200 pounds. Adult does, whose full development ends at 2.5 years when they begin expending their energy on pregnancy and lactating, are 130-140 pounds.

Yet a biologist on a South Texas ranch once told me that he'd never seen a Texas doe field-dress as much as 100 pounds in his 31 years of hunting and only a handful of bucks that reached 130.

On the other hand, in 1981 a 10-point buck killed on the Duluth Indian Reservation in Minnesota was weighed on certified scales at 402 pounds field dressed. Biologists estimated the live weight at 511 pounds—and that only tied the record!

HOW MUCH IS MEAT?

Admit it now, every time a butcher tells you that one box of meat is all that's left of the 150-pound buck you brought him the week before, you suspect he's stowing a little of your venison away for himself—or selling it on the side.

Admittedly, there are a few unscrupulous sorts who aren't above skimming a little venison here and there. But the vast majority of deer cutters are legit.

"Believe me," one veteran deer butcher once told me. "After cutting deer 15-16 hours a day for a month the last thing we want for supper is some of your venison."

"We go home and eat corn flakes and milk."

The truth is most hunters vastly over-estimate the size and therefore the yield of a typical whitetail deer.

My friend, who's been cutting meat for more than 40 years, itemized just what comes in that antlered container and what you can expect to get back.

For comparison we used the average New York-Pennsylvania whitetail, which the respective fish and wildlife staff types say is 120 pounds field-dressed.

"You can figure that the head will weigh eight to 10 pounds, depending on the size of the antlers," said my anonymous friend.

"And the hide will go between 10 and 15 pounds. You'll find that the feet, cut off at the knees, will be one and a half pounds apiece. That should account for about 25-30 pounds total."

If your butcher cuts the meat on a saw, all you're apt to lose after that is 10–12 pounds of ribs and cartilege. But if the carcass is boned, consider the weight discarded with two front shoulders, a pelvis, upper legs and a six-foot vetebrae.

"With an animal that comes in clean and wasn't shot up badly, you might get between 40 and 50 pounds of boned meat."

As if to illustrate the point, he cut up a 134-pound bow-killed buck that night and wrapped it as 57 pounds of boned meat.

Chapter 33
Is Venison Really Heart Healthy?

We all know that venison is heart healthy fare. Very low cholesterol. Very lean. Rich in minerals. It's what nature designed for us to eat.

Well, hang onto your hats gang—particularly those of you who've been selling your spouses on venison because of its low cholesterol content. In actuality it's been found that the cholesterol content of venison from a white-tailed deer can be as much as 50-60 percent HIGHER than beef, depending on the cut. Yeah, higher.

Think about it. You've probably never heard from or read a reputable source that touted the low cholesterol levels in venison. Most people, you see, confuse fat with cholesterol and venison indeed very low in fat.

Since venison, beef and pork all vary in their fat and cholesterol levels, deer hunters frequently ask how these meat compare in their potential effect on the serum cholesterol level, one of the risk factors in cardiovascular disease.

Doctors tell us that the medical recommendations to reduce serum cholesterol by diet include such factors as 1.) reduction in total calories; 2.) reduction in total fat; 3.) reduction in saturated fat; and 4.) reduction in dietary cholesterol.

Not only is venison lower in calories than beef, but boneless venison from does contains fewer calories per 100 grams than meat from bucks. Venison and beef have about the same levels of saturated fatty acids. Venison, however, remains lower in monounsaturated fatty acids and higer in polyunsaturated fatty acids.

A study at North Dakota State University found that venison loin contains slightly more phosphorous, magnesium, iron, copper and manganese than beef loin but lesser amounts of potassium, sodium, calcium and zinc.

The differences, it was felt, probably result from feed sources

A recent study showed that venison from a young doe is lower in calories than that from a buck.

and the ages of the animals. The beef samples used came from animals fed a commercial fattening ration and slaughtered at 18 months. The deer samples were from older animals and obviously there was no control over the deer's food sources.

But not to worry. Venison is still a very healthy red meat. That's why doctors recommend it. Not only is it extremely low in fat, as we said, but venison from a white-tailed deer contains a unique balance of protein, fats and minerals (plus a complete complement of essential amino acids) that provide man with a very complete food item of very high biological value in a very concentrated form.

Because of this whitetail venison has become especially attractive to health-conscious Americans. Those among us who don't like fat and who need to limit their energy intake and lower their saturated fatty acid intake are still able to enjoy a hearty meal of red meat thanks to venison.

According to the American Meat Institute, consumers whose red meat usage is influenced by health considerations grew from 33 percent of all consumers in 1983 to 50 percent in 1985 and is even higher today. Consumer interest in dietary fat, saturated fat and cholesterol grows steadily.

Recent studies suggest that as deer farming practices become more systematic, venison may become the principle meat source for the majority of Americans and possibly some other countries.

"When the speaker and he to whom he speaks do not understand, that is metaphysics."   *—Voltaire*

PART IX:

IN CONCLUSION

Displays like this may be impressive to fellow hunters but trample the sensitivities of non-hunters who could eventually decide our fate.

Chapter 34
The Future Of Hunting

It won't be long before the American hunter becomes an endangered species. Don't scoff; we're on the "threatened" list right now. This statement isn't made for shock effect. It's merely a statement of the inevitable. Sometime before the mid-point of the next century hunting as we know it will be called off due to lack of interest.

Please understand that this prediction isn't from an anti-hunter. The messenger is a hunter, outdoors writer, big game guide—a person whose entire life depends on hunting and the outdoors. He is also a realist.

It's not anti-hunting sentiment killing our pastime. Nor are the reckless or criminal elements in our ranks. Indifference is the poison, according to a landmark study done by Cornell University's Human Dimensions Research Unit in Ithaca, NY.

The study, which involved five sets of national surveys and 20 years worth of data, showed that interest in hunting is dying fast.

Hunting numbers have been in a steady decline for years.

The most recent National Survey of Fishing, Hunting and Wildlife Associated Recreation, conducted in 1991, reported that 14.1 million Americans age 16 and older hunted that year. That was about 7.4 percent of the population. In 1985 the survey counted 16.3 million hunters or 8.4 percent. In 1980 the count was 16.7 million or 9.1 percent.

Although game populations are burgeoning problems such as limited access, less leisure time, disgust with slob hunters, changing societial structure

Public sentiment is changing with each generation.

and competition with other interests has soured those already in the field.

Who among us doesn't know someone who has given up hunting in recent years because they've "killed enough" or because they've lost the urge due to the reaction of their family or friends?

"The future of hunting lies not in the numbers but in the social significance placed on hunting," said Jody Enck, one of the study's researchers, in a talk to the second annual Governor's Symposium on North American Hunting Heritage in South Dakota.

"The decline in hunting numbers represents a decline in an historically important segment of American culture."

Blame the advent of the microchip, the cathode-ray tube, Walt Disney. Blame the ever-growing percentage of single-parent households, the disintegrating family unit and attendant lack of parental influence.

It's a serious problem now and the decline in young people being introduced to hunting will grow exponentially as today's non-hunting youth have children who will be even less likely to appreciate the field.

Bob Delfay, head of the National Shooting Sports Foundation, counters with the fact that there are 1.5 million more young (teen) hunters today than in 1969. He says that the biggest factor in hunting's decline, however, isn't lack of interest or introduction. It's a lack of teen-agers. Far fewer Americans became teens in the last decade, but that's changing fast.

"The Bureau of Census tells us that an average of 250,000 more people per year will turn 13 than did in the last decade," Delfay says. "The Hunter Education Association says that the trend has already begun with a modest increase in participation over the last couple of years."

Time will tell if those new teens will have an impact or venture into areas other than hunting. The recent trend has been toward the latter.

Consider also that women and minorities are the two fastest-growing influence groups in this country. Women (51 percent of the population) make up less than 2 percent of the hunting population and minorities (25 percent of all Americans) are barely measureable in hunting terms. Fully 53 percent of today's hunters live in rural environments while 75 percent of the overall population lives in cities.

Hunting is probably doomed, but its economic impact on society will keep it alive for a while, and growing interest from females will also help slow the decay. Figures from the National Sporting Goods Retailers Association show the number of women hunting tripled from about 640,000 to nearly 2 million. Female participation in shooting sports shows 1.5 million women shooting shotguns, 3 million shooting rifles and pistols.

"The increased participation by women is certainly encouraging if just for the numbers," Delfay says. "But we feel it is also dramatic evidence that our sports provide appropriate, enjoyable, legitimate activities with definite place in modern society."

The industry may see hunting keeping its place in modern society, but the rest of society apparently doesn't. Consider, for instance, the spreading of urban mentality to the suburbs—hunting habitat. More and more wildlife management decisions are being made at the ballot box rather than by professionals. The urban population and its values are oozing outward, replacing rural folks who sell out because they can no longer afford the taxes to keep the family farm.

This is a culture for whom meat is rendered painlessly between Styrofoam and cellophane. For whom water comes from the faucet. For whom wildlife is bird feeder, a 100-foot plot of Chemlawn and a running skirmish with family of raccoons over the garbage. Too many fail to perceive humans as being part of the natural process. They are appalled when the "mean" coyote takes a neighbor's cat, or the "awful" hawk snatches chickadee at bird feeder.

Despite their clearly skewed and grossly innaccurate view of nature, any of these people of voting age are today's wildlife and environmental managers. The uninitiated are making wildlife conservation and environmental decisions at the ballot box and it's a big part of what is wrong with America's outdoors.

By the turn of the century virtually all private land in the east will be posted. Hunters' alternatives will be public land, fee hunting or knowing someone.

Hunting is an experience. It's something that you are led to and share with another. It's not something that can be judged accurately or fairly from a distance.

When a non-hunter looks at hunting he or she sees only the killing. That image overrides the necessity of that death from a management viewpoint; the inevitability of the death from a natural viewpoint. To the uninitiated that death overrides the fact that hunters and fishermen provide more than 80 percent of the funding for fish and wildlife programs today.

We know that without conservation efforts founded and funded by hunters species such as the white-tailed deer, wild turkey, wood-duck, Canada goose, pronghorn antelope, etc., would all be extinct today. The non-hunter cares only about the animal he or she sees, not the plight of a species. Who provided the habitat and protection for that animal is irrelevant.

We can cite these conservation success stories, how much the economy is stimulated by hunting-related revenues, even how effectively modern game laws work in the conservation of species. We can assure them that hunters, more than most, care deeply about the ecosystem integrity and balance and global environment.

Those statements are perfectly true. But they are totally irrelevant to the question at hand. For the non-hunters are not asking whether hunting is an effective management tool, whether it's economically advisable or whether hunters love and appreciate nature. Instead they're asking "Is it morally right to kill animals for sport?"

That answer, in the vast majority of cases, is going to be "no."

It won't do to charge our opponents with scientific ignorance or biological naivete. These are not questions of science. Nor will charges of emotionalism quiet the accusers, since emotions play an integral and valid part in judgements and moral development.

A 1990 Gallup Poll showed that only 21 percent of the population supported a total ban on hunting while 77 percent either "somewhat opposed" or "strongly opposed" a total ban. The poll was commissioned by the National Shooting Sports Foundation. Previous national surveys by the U.S. Fish and Wildlife Service found similar opposition to a total ban on hunting. But it must be noted that the same USFW survey also found a 62 percent opposition to sport hunting for deer and 80 percent opposition to trophy hunting, seen as recreational killing.

Big Buck contests, magazines touting of trophy hunting, gaudy displays of defunct game animals and other senseless trampling of public sensitivities only fuels those judgement-forming emotions mentioned earlier. And while anti-hunting organizations aren't a major factor right now, they're getting louder and aren't adverse to twisting the situation to gain followers.

The annual live pigeon shoot at Hegins, Pa., is protested by anti-hunters and gains huge media attention. Anti-hunters use it as ammunition against legitimate sport hunters.

I once told the Friends of Animals' head (now with the Humane Society of the U.S.) Wayne Pacelle that a live bird shoot is to legitimate hunting what prostitution is to making love.

"I know that," he said with a knowing smile. "And you know that. But 80 percent of the American public can easily see them intertwined."

One renowned survey of bowhunters showed that 51 percent of all deer struck with an arrow were not recovered. When that figure appeared in a local newspaper a representative of an archery club called me to protest. That isn't be accurate, he said. We took a poll in our club and found the figure to be much lower.

Well, I told him, in my experience as a hunting guide and with rank-and-file bowhunters over the years that 51 percent figure was very, very conservative. All it takes to be a bowhunter is a license. Responsibility and skill are not taken into consideration.

Yes, we do have problems in our sport. And we have to address them before the anti-hunters do. The problem is that the antis are generally represented by a celebrity or a Ivy League-educated, well-groomed, handsome, articulate, experienced professional. Our side is too often represented by an Average Joe trying to enjoy himself on his day off when a mike gets thrust in his face.

Public perception is everything in our society and we're simply losing the tug-of-war to the Disney syndrome. We'll never be able to justify killing, regardless of the reasons or result. Yes, it is a purely human notion that death is the worst possible scenario. But it is humans who are making the judgement.

We can postpone the inevitable through educational programs; hunting apprenticeships, political lobbying—but we're not passing the torch. And, like the wildlife we cherish, we hunters are even losing our habitat.

Rural America, the bastion of pro-hunting sentiment, is slowly rotting. There's a definite invasion today of affluent urban types into rural areas looking for self-defined country lifestyle. Unfortunately these people—known as "rurbanites"—all too often still implore urban attitudes and values and expect urban emenities.

The resulting conflict often tears apart the fabric of rural communities and destroys the nature of the very country experience these people sought.

A friend, Bruce Matthews (head of the Coalition for Education in the Outdoors) likens the situation to the difference between a digital watch and dial watch. A digital watch shows you only the moment at hand while a dial displays a sense of knowing where you've been and where you're going. The rurbanite, according to Matthews, is the digital watch, aware only of the present. The rural native, however, has a sense of who and what came before and a hope for the future.

The rurbanite often doesn't hunt or fish and may close his land and attitude to them. These are the new stewards of wildlife since their financial clout can make a once-rural area too expensive for the rooted rural offspring to stay.

The rural mind appreciates the interworking of man and wild things and hunting and fishing's role—but has a decreasing say in management. The answer to this problem, Matthews feels, is outdoor education. He doesn't mean an environmental chapter in the earth science class but rather an environmental theme throughout all curriculum.

"We can't solve environmental problems unless we understand the socio-cultural dimension, which is social studies," Matthews points out.

Unfortunately that interdiscipinary theory isn't popular in today's compartmentalized educational structure.

"But teaching environmental education without using the outdoors is like licking a popsicle through the wrapper," Matthews said. "You can't sense the soul of the experience.

"Those little green pledges on earth day don't connect people with the land. Hunting, fishing and trapping do and we have to educate people to that fact."

We can either do something about it now or simply give up and enjoy hunting while it lasts.

Chapter 35
State Game Departments

(HS) Denotes proof of hunter safety certification required for licensing.

ALABAMA

Alabama Department of Conservation and Natural Resources, Division of Game and Fish, 64 N. Union St., Montgomery, AL 36130. Telephone: 205–242–3465.

ALASKA

Alaska Department of Fish and Game, Division of Wildlife Conservation, Box 25526, Juneau, AK 99802. Telephone: 907–485–4190.

ARIZONA

Arizona Game and Fish Department, 2221 West Greenway Road, Phoenix, AZ 85023. Telephone: 602–942–3000. (HS)

ARKANSAS

Arkansas Game and Fish Commission, No. 2 Natural Resources Drive, Little Rock, AR 72205. Telephone: 501–223–6300. (HS)

CALIFORNIA

California Department of Fish and Game, Wildlife Management Division, 1416 Ninth St., Sacramento, CA 95814. Telephone: 916–653–7664. (HS)

COLORADO

Colorado Division of Wildlife, 6060 Broadway, Denver, CO 80216. Telephone: 303–297–1192. (HS)

CONNECTICUT

Connecticut Department of Environmental Protection, Wildlife Division, 79 Elm St., Hartford, CT 06106–5127. Telephone: 203–424–3011. (HS)

DELAWARE
Delaware Department of Natural Resources and Environmental Control, Division of Fish & Wildlife, 89 Kings Highway, PO Box 1401, Dover, DE 19903. Telephone: 302–739–5297. (HS)

FLORIDA
Florida Game and Fresh Water Fish Commission, 620 South Meridian St., Tallahassee, FL 32399–1600. Telephone: 904–488–4676. (HS)

GEORGIA
Georgia Department of Natural Resources, Wildlife Resources Division, 2070 U.S. Highway 278 SE, Social Circle, GA 30279. Telephone: 404–918–6416. (HS)

HAWAII
Hawaii Department of Land and Natural Resources, Division of Forestry and Wildlife, 1151 Punchbowl St., Honolulu, HI 96813. Telephone: 808–587–0166. (HS)

IDAHO
Idaho Department of Fish and Game, PO Box 25, 600 South Walnut St., Boise, ID 83707. Telephone: 208–334–3700. (HS)

ILLINOIS
Illinois Department of Conservation, Division of Wildlife Resources, Lincoln Tower Plaza, 524 S. Second St., Springfield, IL 62701–1787. Telephone: 217–782–6384. (HS)

INDIANA
Indiana Department of Natural Resources, Division of Fish and Wildlife, 402 W. Washington, Room W273, Indianapolis, IN 46204. Telephone: 317–232–4080.

IOWA
Iowa Department of Natural Resources, Wallace State Office Bldg., Des Moines, IA 50319. Telephone: 515–281–5145. (HS)

KANSAS
Kansas Department of Wildlife and Parks, 512 Southeast 25th Ave., Pratt, KS 67124. Telephone: 316–672–5911. (HS)

KENTUCKY
Kentucky Department of Fish and Wildlife Resources, Frankfort, KY 40601. Telephone: 502–564–4336.

LOUISIANA
Louisiana Department of Wildlife and Fisheries, PO Box 9800, Baton Rouge, LA 70898–9000. Telephone: 504–765–2925. (HS)

MAINE
Maine Department of Inland Fisheries and Wildlife, 284 State St., State House Station 41, Augusta, ME 04333. Telephone: 207–287–2871. (HS)

MARYLAND
Maryland Department of Natural Resources, Wildlife Division, Tawes State Office Bldg., E-1, 580 Taylor Ave., Annapolis, MD 21401. Telephone: 410–974–3195. (HS)

MASSACHUSETTS
Massachusetts Division of Fisheries and Wildlife, 100 Cambridge St., Boston, MA 02202. Telephone: 617–727–3151.

MICHIGAN
License Control, Michigan Department of Natural Resources, Box 30028, Lansing, MI 48909. Telephone: 517–373–1204. (HS)

MINNESOTA
Minnesota Department of Natural Resources, Division of Fish and Wildlife, Box 7, DNR Bldg., 500 Lafayette St., St. Paul, MN 55155. Telephone: 612–296–6157. (HS)

MISSISSIPPI
Mississippi Department of Wildlife, Fisheries and Parks, PO Box 451, Jackson, MS 39205. Telephone: 602–362–9212. (HS)

MISSOURI
Missouri Department of Conservation, Wildlife Programs Supervisor, PO Box 180, Jefferson City, MO 65102. Telephone: 314–751–4115. (HS)

MONTANA
Montana Department of Fish, Wildlife and Parks, 1420 East Sixth Ave., Helena, MT 59620. Telephone: 406–444–2535. (HS)

NEBRASKA
Nebraska Game and Parks Commission, PO Box 30370, Lincoln, NE 68503-0370. Telephone: 402–471–0641. (HS)

NEVADA
Nevada Division of Wildlife, PO Box 10678, 1100 Valley Road, Reno, NV 89520. Telephone: 702–688–1500. (HS)

NEW HAMPSHIRE
New Hampshire Fish and Game Department, 2 Hazen Drive, Concord, NH 03301. Telephone: 603–271–3421. (HS)

NEW JERSEY
New Jersey Department of Environmental Protection and Energy, Division of Fish, Game and Wildlife, CN-400, Trenton, NJ 08625–0400. Telephone: 609–292–2965. (HS)

NEW MEXICO
New Mexico Department of Game and Fish, PO Box 25112, Santa Fe, NM 87504–5112. Telephone: 505–827–7911. (HS)

NEW YORK
New York Department of Environmental Conservation, Fish & Wildlife Division, 50 Wolf Road, Albany, NY 12233. Telephone: 518–457–5400. (HS)

NORTH CAROLINA
North Carolina Wildlife Resources Commission, 512 N. Salisbury St., Raleigh, NC 27604–1188. Telephone: 919–733–3391. (HS)

NORTH DAKOTA
North Dakota Game and Fish Department, 100 N. Bismarck Expressway, Bismarck, ND 58501. Telephone: 701–221–6300. (HS)

OHIO
Ohio Department of Natural Resources, Division of Wildlife, 1840 Belcher Drive, G-3, Columbus, OH 43244–1329. Telephone: 614–265–6300. (HS)

OKLAHOMA
Oklahoma Department of Wildlife Conservation, 1801 N. Lincoln, Oklahoma City, OK 73105. Telephone: 405–521–3851. (HS)

OREGON
Oregon Department of Fish and Wildlife, PO Box 59, Portland, OR 97207. Telephone: 503–229–5454. (HS)

PENNSYLVANIA
Pennsylvania Game Commission, 2001 Elmerton Ave., Harrisburg, PA 17110–9797. Telephone: 717–787–6286. (HS)

RHODE ISLAND
Rhode Island Department of Environmental Management, Division of Fish, Wildlife and Estuarine Resources, PO Box 218, West Kingston, RI 02892. Telephone: 401–789–0281. (HS)

SOUTH CAROLINA
South Carolina Department of Natural Resources, PO Box 167, Columbia, SC 29202. Telephone: 803–734–3886.

SOUTH DAKOTA
South Dakota Department of Game, Fish and Parks, 523 E. Capitol, Pierre, SD 57501. Telephone: 605–773–3485. (HS)

TENNESSEE
Tennessee Wildlife Resources Agency, PO Box 40747, Nashville, TN 37204. Telephone: 615–781–6500. (HS)

TEXAS
Texas Parks and Wildlife Department, 4200 Smith School Road, Austin, TX 78744. Telephone: 800–792–1112.

UTAH
Utah Division of Wildlife Resources, 1596 West North Temple, Salt Lake City, UT 84116. Telephone: 801–538–4700. (HS)

VERMONT
Vermont Fish and Wildlife Department, Waterbury, VT 05676. Telephone: 802–241–3700. (HS)

VIRGINIA
Virginia Department of Game and Inland Fisheries, 4010 W Broad St., Richmond, VA 23230-1104. Telephone: 804–367–1000.

WASHINGTON
Washington Department of Fish and Wildlife, 600 Capitol Way N., Olympia, WA 98501. Telephone: 206–753–5700.

WEST VIRGINIA
West Virginia Division of Natural Resources, Wildlife Resources Section, State Capitol Complex, Bldg. 3, 1900 Kanawha Blvd., Charleston, WV 25305. Telephone: 304–558–2771.

WISCONSIN
Wisconsin Bureau of Wildlife Management, Box 7921, Madison, WI 53707. Telephone: 608–266–1877. (HS)

WYOMING
Wyoming Game and Fish Department, Cheyenne, WY 82002. Telephone: 307–777–4601. (HS)

CANADA

ALBERTA
Alberta Environmental Protection, Fish and Wildlife Services, 9945 108th St., Edmonton, Alberta T5K 2G6. Telephone: 403–427–6729.

BRITISH COLUMBIA
British Columbia Ministry of the Environment, Lands and Parks, Wildlife Branch, Parliament Buildings, 730 Blanshard St., Victoria, British Columbia V8V 1X5. Telephone: 604–387–9737. (HS)

MANITOBA
Manitoba Department of Natural Resources, 1495 St. James St., Box 22, Winnipeg, Manitoba R3H 0W9. Telephone: 204–945–6784. (HS)

NEW BRUNSWICK
New Brunswick Department of Natural Resources and Energy, Fish and Wildlife Branch, PO Box 6000, Fredericton, New Brunswick E3B 5H1. Telephone: 506–453–2440. (HS)

NEWFOUNDLAND AND LABRADOR
Newfoundland Department of Environment and Lands, Wildlife Division, PO Box 8700, St. John's Newfoundland A1B 4J6. Telephone: 709–729–2815. (HS)

NORTHWEST TERRITORIES
Department of Renewable Resources, Government of the Northwest Territories, Scotia Centre 600, 5102–50 Ave., Yellowknife, NT X1A 3S8. Telephone: 403–920–8716. (HS)

NOVA SCOTIA
Nova Scotia Department of Natural Resources, PO Box 698, Halifax, Nova Scotia B3J 2T9. Telephone: 902–424–5254. (HS)

ONTARIO
Ontario Ministry of Natural Resources Information Centre, 900 Bay St., Room MI-73 Macdonald Block, Toronto, Ontario M7A 2C1. Telephone: 416–314–2000. (HS)

PRINCE EDWARD ISLAND
Prince Edward Island Department of Environmental Resources, Fish and Wildlife Division, PO Box 2000, Charlottetown, Prince Edward Island, C1A 7N8. Telephone: 902–368–4683. (HS)

QUEBEC
Quebec Ministere Environnement et Faune, 150 boul. Rene-Levesque Est, 4e etage, Quebec City, Quebec G1R 4Y1. Telephone: 418–643–3127. (HS)

SASKATCHEWAN
Saskatchewan Environment and Resource Management, 3211 Albert St., Regina, Saskatchewan S4S 5W6. Telephone: 306–787–9034.

YUKON TERRITORY
Yukon Territory Department of Renewable Resources, Field Services Branch, PO Box 2703, Whitehorse, Yukon Territory Y1A 2C6. Telephone: 403–667–5221.

THE END

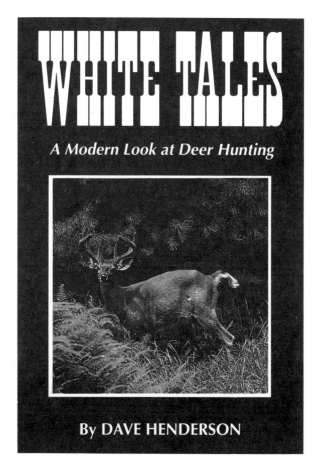

WHITE TALES

A Modern Look at Deer Hunting

By DAVE HENDERSON

Additional copies of *Whitetales* are available for
$12.95 plus shipping and handling.